CNN's
COLD WAR
Documentary

Issues and Controversy

CNN's COLD WAR Documentary

Issues and Controversy

Edited by
ARNOLD BEICHMAN

HOOVER INSTITUTION PRESS
Stanford University Stanford, California

Hoover Institution Press Publication No. 466
Copyright © 2000 by the Board of Trustees of the
    Leland Stanford Junior University

Cover photos © Corbis/Bettmann. Main photo: Brandenburg Gate, in Berlin,
seen through barbed wire. Inset photo: Soviet missiles parade past Kremlin.

First printing, 2000
06   05   04   03   02   01   00   9   8   7   6   5   4   3   2   1

Manufactured in the United States of America
The paper used in this publication meets the minimum requirements
of American National Standard for Information Sciences—Permanence
of Paper for Printed Library Materials, ANSI Z39.48–1984. ⊗

Library of Congress Cataloging-in-Publication Data
CNN's Cold war documentary : issues and controversy
        p.   cm.
    ISBN 0-8179-9742-3 (alk. paper)
    1. Cold War.   2. World politics—1945–   3. Cable News Network.
D843 .C5673   2000
070.1'95—dc21   99-037156

Contents

PART TWO   OP-EDS AND BRIEF ARTICLES

Foreword

Most wars end with a ceremony of surrender, a carefully choreographed event that the triumphant combatants insist is especially necessary—given the great price paid—to declare a winner and a loser for all the world to see. In contrast, the Cold War, to the world's great fortune, ended with a whimper, not a bang, and no comparable surrender ceremony neatly identified winners and losers in the forty-five-year contest that kept two superpowers in conflict and the world on edge.

Indeed, the Cold War is not at all like most wars the world has known. Defined by an uneasy peace, all the while never more than thirty minutes away from nuclear-tipped Armageddon; decided not in the end by a direct engagement of arms but by the collapse of one of its combatants; waged in the realm of ideas and ideology and not simply arms and arsenals, the Cold War's end occasioned not clarity, but more controversy—as a small army of public servants, political scientists, historians, activists, and academics instantly became entrenched over "what it all meant." Not surprisingly, CNN's decision to undertake a twenty-four-part history of the conflict became a defining moment that accentuated the dialogue over the Cold War—guaranteeing controversy even before the first episode went on the air.

Not to say that there is significant controversy over the Cold War's outcome. Indeed, as Sir Jeremy Isaacs—executive producer of CNN's *Cold War* series and, in this volume, target of many essayists who fault the CNN series as being biased toward the Soviets and against the United States and the West—succinctly puts it: "The right side won." Even so, questions abound: If the West won—at what harm to itself? Did the war itself bring out the best in the West—or its worst? Who is responsible—in terms of action-reaction—for the flashpoints that very nearly made the Cold War dangerously and deadly hot? Such questions are anything but academic and explain the passion evident in the pages that follow. Is the CNN series, as columnist Charles Krauthammer says, a moral affront to the West's resolve, dedicated to a "relentless attempt to find moral equivalence between the two sides"? Or, as executive producer Sir Jeremy Isaacs says, is CNN's *Cold War* "simply and directly, without gloss or spin — a guide you can trust to the story of our time"?

Surely John Lewis Gaddis, the eminent historian who served as consultant to the CNN series (though not, as he is careful to differentiate, the book accompanying the series) is correct when he notes that we can't rerun history the way we can repeat a chemistry experiment, to see if we've got it right. The quest for an entirely "accurate" account of any historic event will elude us always — a fact that nevertheless does not absolve us of trying to wring truth from the past, for the sake of the future. As befitting the Cold War itself — a clash between two systems, two civilizations animated by warring worldviews — many of the essays in this book are pointed and even personal in the arguments they make. The Cold War may be over, but the warring dialogue about what the Cold War means has only just begun. History doesn't get any hotter than this.

Yet the fact that serious people seriously disagree does not mean that the extremes cancel each other out, leaving the truth to be found in some mushy middle ground. Nor is the Cold War an abstraction onto which we impose our own reality. When it comes to the defining conflict of the twentieth century, there is a truth to be told, and it is a truth very much worth knowing — lest mankind ever be sentenced to repeating the history of which we are ignorant. Clearly, a period so harrowing to live through is worth arguing over.

Isaacs and his colleagues have conceived and dramatized an undertaking of epic proportions — interviews with more than five hundred participants, review of millions of feet of film as well as archival materials from previously unavailable sources in the West as well as the Soviet bloc. Because the CNN series' coproducer Martin Smith scoured the archives at the Fulton, Missouri, museum commemorating Winston Churchill's famed Iron Curtain speech, we have now in one episode an 8-mm "home movie," which had languished in an unmarked film canister all these years, that allows us to recapture the immediacy of Churchill's warning. Because the CNN team pressed to gain access to newly opened archives in Moscow and elsewhere in the old Soviet bloc, we can see what that Iron Curtain obscured from view: The series includes, for instance, riveting film footage of the KGB's arrest, interrogation, and trial of the CIA's most valuable Soviet spy, identified to the Soviets by Aldrich Ames. Because, as Sir Jeremy Isaacs notes, Ted Turner pressed forward with uncommon speed on the Cold War project, interviews with aging eyewitnesses to key Cold War events were obtained that would otherwise have been lost to history. For instance, when the Cold War producers approached Kennedy aide McGeorge Bundy about an interview, Bundy consulted his contemporary, former CBS news executive Fred Friendly. Friendly persuaded Bundy to do the interview, which he did, only to die three weeks later (shortly after, Friendly, too, passed away). A bit of good luck, to be sure — but as sports fans know, the best teams make their own luck. If the same goes for documentary series, CNN's *Cold War* team deserves kudos for digging deeper and pushing harder to bring to the public points of view and pieces of evidence we did not possess.

There's a popular saying in our video age: Don't just watch the movie, read the book. This book gathers commentary about how we should view an important time in our history. It is important to understand the dialogue that prevails over "what it all meant." It is healthy to have perspective about the "movie" as we seek certain truths about such times. We should not necessarily depend on one treatment as a description of truth and worthy of sole inference. With this said, when you have finished reading the war of words in the pages that follow, you may well watch and read CNN's *Cold War* with an eye for controversy and come to your own conclusions about the conflict that, more than any other, gave shape to the twentieth century and, in so doing, defined our prospects in the twenty-first.

John Raisian
Director, Hoover Institution

Introduction:
The Cold War Was a Just War

Arnold Beichman

Arnold Beichman, a research fellow at the Hoover Institution, Stanford University, is coauthor of *Yuri Andropov: New Challenge to the West*, author of *The Long Pretense: Soviet Treaty Diplomacy from Lenin to Gorbachev*, and a columnist for the *Washington Times*.

*What is the use of lying, when truth, well distributed,
serves the same purpose?*
                              —W. E. Forster[1]

John Stuart Mill wrote, "On all great subjects much remains to be said," and of none is this more true than of the cold war.[2]

This book, a collection of previously published articles,[3] is for the most part highly critical of the documentary produced by the British filmmaker Sir Jeremy Isaacs at the instance of Ted Turner, founder of Cable News Network (CNN). In keeping with John Stuart Mill's stricture, I have also decided to include responses by defenders of the documentary, including those from the two eminent historians who served as consultants to the CNN project as well as from Sir Jeremy himself.

By including the viewpoint of the film's producers, I do not intend to imply acceptance of the old saw that there are three sides to any question — your side, my side, and the right side. I passionately believe that the twenty-four-episode documentary and the accompanying "teacher's aid" textbook

1. Said about the Russian diplomat Count Nicholas Ignatiev, after a conversation with him, by the British statesman W. E. Forster. In T. Weymss Reid, "Life" ii (1888), page 167. Quoted in *The Times* (London), March 18, 1989.
2. I am, of course, paraphrasing the opening sentence of Walter Bagehot's masterwork *The English Constitution* (Cornell University Press, 1966), p. 39.
3. With the exception of three essays by Richard Pipes, Robert Conquest, and John Lewis Gaddis commissioned specially for this volume.

are deeply flawed as history, particularly as a history of a war of ideas, which, happily for mankind, never became a war of annihilation.

The forty-five-year cold war was, and I do not regard this as oversimplification, a conflict in which one side was morally right and the other side morally wrong. Such a view, of course, is widely accepted in thinking about World War II and Adolf Hitler. There is no reason why Josef Stalin, a master genocidist, should be regarded as morally superior to Hitler. I deride the notion purveyed by the producers of the documentary that such former Soviet leaders as Lenin and Gorbachev had virtuous intentions.

My greatest concern, and one that has motivated me to produce this book, is that the distorted vision that informs the Turner-Isaacs documentary and the accompanying textbook is going to land in classrooms all over the country for years and come to be accepted as historical truth. I hope that our book will be read by school boards, school principals, teachers, especially high school history teachers, as demonstrating that the cold war was not merely a struggle between a pair of equally demented gorillas whose snarls and wild swings endangered world peace. In the cold war, the enemy of freedom was communism, despite its propaganda claims to be idealism in action, a claim that the Turner-Isaacs documentary and textbook appear at times to accept as valid.

I hope that the contents of this book will demonstrate that the cold war was as much a "just war" as was World War II. The free world triumph over Marxism-Leninism is something we and our children can be proud of because that triumph, overnight in one fell swoop without a shot fired, brought down the Berlin Wall—November 9, 1999, is the tenth anniversary of that historic event—and liberated millions of people in Eastern and Central Europe as well as within the Soviet Union itself.

COLD WAR

PART ONE
Essays

Twenty-four Lies about the Cold War

Gabriel Schoenfeld

Gabriel Schoenfeld is the senior editor of *Commentary* magazine. Reprinted from the April 1999 *Commentary* with permission. All rights reserved.

The Iron Curtain came down in 1989. Two years later, the Soviet Union itself was no more, and neither was the cold war—a conflict that, for well over four decades, had divided the world into two hostile camps.

In the course of those decades, wherever Marxism-Leninism had been planted by force of arms, millions of people were deliberately murdered or spent their best years in prison camps. Those not imprisoned lived constricted, fear-filled lives. In hot wars involving the superpowers in remote corners of the world, from Angola to Afghanistan to Nicaragua, the human toll was great on both sides. More than fifty-four thousand Americans died in the Korean War; another fifty-eight thousand died defending South Vietnam.

Not surprisingly, for a conflict of such duration and magnitude, the causes of the dispute have themselves been a subject of controversy—not only between the two adversaries but within the world of elite American opinion. For the first half of the cold war, the dominant view in this country, including among most liberals and intellectuals, held the USSR to be the clear aggressor. The Kremlin's brutal behavior, especially in Europe, posed an immense challenge to freedom; hence the policy of "firm containment," enunciated in 1947 by George F. Kennan and designed "to confront the Russians with unalterable counterforce at every point where they show signs of encroaching upon the interest of a peaceful and stable world."

But by the mid-1960s, as containment drew the United States deeper and deeper into Vietnam, both the policy itself and the view of the USSR it presupposed came under sharp attack. Self-proclaimed "revisionists" insisted that the cold war was nothing more than a cruelly absurd battle between two empires, equally reprehensible, equally thirsty for markets,

power, and territory. Some went further, casting the United States alone
as the prime offender; Moscow, argued such scholars as Gabriel Kolko
and Richard J. Barnet, wanted nothing more than to preserve the status
quo, while Washington, in the grip of an irrational anticommunism, was
pursuing an expansionist agenda in the name of a spurious "freedom." As
the Vietnam War dragged on, politicizing American intellectual life to an
unprecedented degree, the revisionist view became deeply entrenched
among academic and mass media elites.

Since the dissolution of the communist world, however, at least a
partial reversal of opinion has been under way. The historical revelations
flowing in a torrent from the East, all confirming the older understanding
of the origins of the cold war and the nature of the Soviet regime, have
had the effect of putting revisionism on the defensive. A landmark in the
process was the publication in 1997 of We Now Know, a comprehensive
reexamination of cold war history by the dean of American diplomatic
historians, John Lewis Gaddis.[1] Drawing on material from once top-secret
archives in Eastern Europe and the USSR, the memoirs of ranking
communist officials, and the research of other Western scholars, Gaddis
refuted the revisionist case point by point.

Given this accomplishment, it came as welcome news that Gaddis
would be serving as a principal adviser to a comprehensive series on the
Soviet-American confrontation to be produced by the television network
CNN. For that network, under the direction of its founder and chief
executive, Ted Turner, has over the years acquired a well-deserved reputation for standing to the left of even "mainstream" media. In fact, in June
1998, just three months before Cold War was scheduled to start, CNN
aired a "news-magazine" program, Valley of Death, falsely charging that
the U.S. military had used poison gas to kill American defectors during
the Vietnam War.[2] Although CNN (under a hail of criticism and the threat
of lawsuits) repudiated the show and fired its producers, the episode raised
questions about the internal journalistic culture that would allow a highly
improbable, highly anti-American story on the air unchecked.

1. I reviewed this book in the September 1997 Commentary.
2. See "Nerve Gas, Lies, and Videotape," by Joshua Muravchik in the September
1998 Commentary.

In scope and ambition *Cold War* is certainly a far cry from *Valley of Death*. The program that Ted Turner envisioned as "the most important production in [CNN's] eighteen-year history" was conceived not as a twenty-minute news magazine but as an immense forty-part series (later scaled back to twenty-four) in which the viewer would be propelled through the frightening shoals and straits of the cold war in chronological sequence. Sir Jeremy Isaacs, the man behind the outstanding British World War II series of twenty-five years ago, *The World at War*, was brought in as executive producer and given a generous $12 million budget to do the job.

Under Isaacs's direction, a small army of production associates and assistants was assembled in London and then dispatched to more than thirty countries to secure interviews with eyewitnesses to pivotal events. Over the course of three years, more than five hundred key historical figures were recorded talking about what they had seen and heard. Included were ranking government officials like Anatoly Dobrynin and Robert S. McNamara; observer-participants like Sergei Khrushchev, son of Nikita, and the historian and former diplomat Robert C. Tucker; and "ordinary" people ranging from Islamic guerrillas in Afghanistan to rank-and-file Communist Party members in France.

Combing archives around the world, the producers also compiled 8,500 film clips of varying degrees of significance. In all, more than a million feet of film were brought to London to be weighed for possible use. In line with Ted Turner's desire for an "international perspective," by which he meant that *Cold War* should strive to show the conflict from the viewpoint of its major protagonists, a team of scholars, including Gaddis as well as prominent historians from the University of London, the Institute of Universal History in Moscow, and other major research institutions in Europe, was recruited to offer a diversity of views and to "check every frame [of the film] and read every syllable" of the scripts for accuracy.

The resulting show, which began airing in September 1998 and concluded in April 1999, has received both praise and criticism. I shall turn to the reactions in due course, but perhaps the first thing to say about *Cold War* is that some aspects of it are unquestionably excellent. Kenneth Branagh, the Irish actor and director, provides what is essential in the narrator of a documentary of this type: a voice that pronounces every word with unwavering authority. The score, by the British composer Carl Davis, is suitably ominous and dramatic. And, more centrally, a number of the interviews with notable cold war personages leave indelible impressions. Listening, for example, to Aldrich Ames, the American who served as a Soviet "mole" inside the CIA, explain his betrayal of the United States while a ghastly video shows his most significant Soviet victim being arrested and interrogated in Moscow, distinctly raises one's consciousness of human evil.

In what it enables us to see, in the Ames case and in the thousands upon thousands of other images that scroll across the twenty-four segments of the show, *Cold War* truly is a magnificent achievement; if it is not "jaw-dropping," as CNN's publicity machine claims, at more than a few moments it comes close. The assistants who labored in tropical and frigid climes around the world succeeded in assembling a collection of images — both still and moving — that captures many crucial junctures of the momentous conflict, some of them long forgotten, many of them hitherto unseen.

The cold war, *Cold War* serves to remind us, had terrifying moments of heat. There is, for example, riveting footage of East Germans making their way over the primitive barriers that the Communists erected to divide Berlin in 1961, some of them pausing momentarily to extricate clothing and flesh that had become snagged on the barbed wire. And there are even more arresting stills of a young man, Peter Fechter, who attempted to escape to the West, was fired on by East German guards, and, stranded atop the Berlin Wall, bled to death over a period of hours within yards of West Berliners too fearful to help.

There is also, to take still another example, a formerly top-secret clip of the great Soviet rocket disaster of 1960. Nikita Khrushchev, in a hurry to test fire the SS-7 intercontinental ballistic missile, pushed his military to the corner-cutting point and beyond. With Marshal Mitrofan Nedelin, commander of the USSR's strategic rocket forces, and other top brass assembled on the launch pad, something went catastrophically awry; the liquid fuel in the rocket engine ignited prematurely. The camera shows scientists and military officers running from the blast, but not fast enough, and then being incinerated on the spot. All that was ever found of Marshal Nedelin were his medals.

In its march through contemporary history, *Cold War* also offers feeds from such disparate eruptions as the Korean War (bombs pounding innocent civilians), Romania in communism's death throes (President Nicolae Ceauşescu and his wife struggling with their executioners as they are prepared for the firing squad), and the Soviet incursion into Afghanistan (guerrillas stalking and then blowing up a Soviet armored personnel carrier, with soldiers dying horribly on the ground). In the brutality depicted in these pictures, we are reminded of the staggering costs in human life that the cold war imposed. And again and again we are also reminded that many more could have perished, that life itself could have been erased from the face of the earth: *Cold War* contains numerous shots of A- and H-bombs exploding terrifyingly, complete with flashes brighter than a thousand suns and enormous plumes of radioactive dust billowing into the atmosphere.

The pictures contained in *Cold War* are immensely compelling. In the end, however, we demand more from a historical documentary than awe-inspiring images. How does *Cold War* stack up as a work of history?

The question is of no ordinary consequence. Apart from being screened before a worldwide television audience, the series is designed to introduce the topic of the cold war into the high school curriculum of the United States. Already endorsed by the National Council for the Social Studies, the twenty-four one-hour segments are now being distributed to schools on videocassette tapes for a nominal fee. CNN has also produced an extensive study guide and an interactive CD-ROM to help educators steer students through the East-West struggle. In addition, it is offering a lavishly illustrated companion volume, suitable for use as a textbook in schools, in which it is noted that John Lewis Gaddis had a leading hand.[3]

The critical reception of *Cold War*, as I have already noted, has been mixed. *Time*, weighing in in favor, called it "documentary television at its best" — "serious, thorough, and absorbing." The *New York Times* reviewer praised it as "gripping straightforward history . . . more intense than a John le Carré thriller." From some quarters, however, the words have been less kind, raising an echo of earlier ideological disputes. The *New Republic*

---

3. *Cold War: An Illustrated History, 1945–1991*, companion to the CNN TV series, by Jeremy Isaacs and Taylor Downing. Little, Brown, 438 pp., $39.95.

lambasted the series for presenting the cold war as a "morally unintelligible contest between two equally dangerous superpowers." The historian Ronald Radosh, writing in the *New York Times*, similarly blasted the program for suggesting "a moral equivalence between the Soviet bloc and the democratic Western allies." The columnist Charles Krauthammer has charged that it "often goes beyond mere moral equivalence to cheap anti-Americanism."

For his part, John Lewis Gaddis, also writing in the *Times*, has mounted a vigorous defense. Of the several hundred Yale students for whom he has played the tapes, he asserts, "I see few if any come away convinced that the two sides in this struggle were morally equivalent." The series, Gaddis points out, shows such Soviet atrocities as "the Red Army rapes in Germany in 1945, the crushing of the Hungarian uprising in 1956, the suppression of the Prague Spring in 1968, the invasion of Afghanistan in 1979, and the persecution of dissidents in the Soviet Union and Eastern Europe throughout the cold war." After watching these horrors, most students, says Gaddis, would not only reject the accusation of moral equivalence but find it "laughable."

One problem in sorting out the differences in these opinions is that, as Jeremy Isaacs has observed, "television history is short, by comparison with academic history, on analysis; long on anecdote." Another is that the series, to quote Gaddis, deliberately "did not try to settle old arguments about responsibility for the cold war"; instead, "we tried to allow all kinds of people to tell their stories." It is from these stories, and from the narrator's brief interjections and commentary, that both critics and defenders have fashioned their respective cases.

How to settle the dispute? One avenue might be to supplement a viewing of the film with an examination of the companion volume, which at least makes a stab at what Jeremy Isaacs calls "academic history." Are the moral and intellectual lapses pointed to by critics of the series repaired by the less anecdotal and more systematic approach of the book? Unfortunately, the answer is not at all. To the contrary, the problematic aspects of the film—and there are many—are only magnified in the book, becoming infused with an extreme brand of revisionism. Although one could usefully examine the defects in every one of *Cold War*'s twenty-four segments, a glimpse of how it and its companion volume handle four crucial junctures is enough to provide a flavor of the whole.

Let us begin with the prehistory of the conflict. In the film, we are not told very much about Bolshevism in its early years, but what little there is is almost comic in what it chooses to include, and tragicomic in what it chooses to omit.

The cold war, we learn in "Comrades," the first episode of the series, had its origins after World War I "in a clash of ideologies, Communist and capitalist." The Allies, determined to snuff out the Marxist experiment, sent troops into Russia, thereby convincing Lenin and Stalin "that the West would seize any chance, embrace any ally, in order to destroy Communism." Winston Churchill, then the British secretary of state for war, is presented as a frothing-at-the-mouth anti-Communist, spouting the slogan "Kill the Bolshie! Kiss the Hun!"

Do we get a more nuanced picture from the book? Hardly. We find instead still more anticommunist raving. "Civilization is being completely extinguished over gigantic areas," runs the single quotation, again from Churchill, explaining the British decision to send forces to Russian soil: "Bolsheviks hop and caper like troops of ferocious baboons." All this, the authors protest, about a government that, although "as authoritarian as that of the czars," was making an effort not to wipe out civilization but to renew it. Lenin's "socialist principles were meant to ensure decent education, free health care, common ownership of land, and fairness for all."

Where, in documentary or book, is the mass shooting of innocent civilians taken as hostages during the Red Terror and Russia's civil war? Where are the millions who died in the famine deliberately engineered by Lenin during the period known as War Communism? Where are all the other acts of savagery that, in their totality, made the Russian Revolution such a fitting preface to this century of barbarism? Not a hint of a critical thought about Lenin appears anywhere, only prattling tributes to his "deep commitment to bettering the lives of ordinary Russians."

Nor do matters improve when CNN turns, in the second of the four junctures, to the cold war's more immediate causes in the years following World War II. Here, in a pattern that will recur, the USSR is consistently depicted as weak, inward-looking, and consumed by its own internal stresses, while the United States is cast as warlike, expansionist, and consumed by a senseless fear of communism, Communists, and the USSR.

Thus we learn that Stalin, presiding over a country that lay in ruin, "feared encirclement by the capitalist powers." He grew especially "nervous" when, after 1945, America began "extending its influence and power all over the world" out of an evident determination to create "a free-enterprise Western bloc." This left the USSR with no choice; it "was *forced* to build its own rival bloc" (emphasis added).

Although President Harry Truman "suspected that Stalin was aiming at world domination," in fact, CNN assures us, Soviet aims were not aggressive at all: the USSR was merely seeking a buffer zone. A somewhat more real prospect was that left-wing forces in prostrate Western Europe might triumph via the ballot box. Responding to this menace with an extensive aid program, Truman wrapped his proposal in feverish anticommunism, stating in his historic 1947 address to Congress that "the United States would contain the advance of Communism anywhere on the globe." "This," CNN's narrator pronounces with solemnity, "was the official declaration of the cold war."

If the film suggests that Truman's "declaration of war" was a foolish political ploy that brought horrendous consequences, the book emphasizes America's lack of discernment and its overweening need for an external enemy: "It suited Western interests for public opinion to perceive the Russian position in negative terms." The United States was thus fully primed to react with hysteria to the innocuous but harsh-sounding tics that punctuated Stalin's political rhetoric. On top of everything else, this knee-jerk response was traceable in part to the abysmally low quality of American leadership. Truman, we are told, had a distressing tendency "to see things in clearly defined black and white terms"; he "lacked the patience to weigh up subtleties of argument"; and he was "largely ignorant of foreign affairs." Worst of all, he surrounded himself with men of similarly low capacities, among them General George C. Marshall, who became secretary of state in 1947 and was neither "well informed on foreign affairs" nor eager to learn.

Among Truman's advisers, only Secretary of Commerce Henry Wallace is presented as free of intellectual or character flaws. This advocate of "a more conciliatory line" understood, according to the book, "that the

Russians were only trying to stand up for what they had won at Yalta and Potsdam." And yet, in becoming a "dissenting voice," Wallace was compelled by Truman to resign, an act for which the entire world paid a price since Wallace was the only member of Truman's cabinet to grasp that "for America to take a tougher line would be to force Stalin to take a tougher line in response."

One hardly knows where to begin with this farrago of inventions. Perhaps the most forceful rebuttal is the one penned by John Lewis Gaddis himself in *We Now Know*. There, Gaddis truthfully explains the conflict's origins in terms diametrically opposed to those offered on the program to which he served as adviser. The U.S.-Soviet confrontation, he writes, had its roots not in anything America did or failed to do in the diplomatic, economic, or military realm, but almost entirely in the peculiar characteristics of the Soviet tyrant and his regime. "It was Stalin's disposition to wage cold wars," notes Gaddis in *We Now Know*; "he had done so in one form or another throughout his life." And *"as long as Stalin was running the Soviet Union a cold war was unavoidable"* (emphasis in the original).

In the chaotic aftermath of World War II, Gaddis goes on to state, what the historical record suggests about Stalin's behavior "is not that Stalin had limited objectives, only that he had no timetable" for realizing whatever objectives he had. In the words of his right-hand man, Vyacheslav Molotov, "Our ideology stands for offensive operations when possible, and if not, we wait." It was mainly thanks to Truman's resolve, and to the decisive steps he and Marshall took to demonstrate that resolve—steps that CNN twists into provocative acts of aggression—that Stalin chose to forgo "offensive operations" and spend his energy instead on digesting the European territories that the Red Army had already managed to swallow and subjugating their populations through coercion and naked terror.

As for the halo that appears over the head of Henry Wallace, CNN's book somehow neglects to inform its readers that, when Truman forced him from office, the commerce secretary had already moved well down the path toward an openly pro-Soviet stance. By 1948, when he himself ran for the presidency on the communist-backed Progressive Party ticket, Wallace was defending Stalin's foreign policy in all its manifestations, claiming, for example, without any evidence but in perfect synchrony with

Moscow's line, that the communist takeover in Czechoslovakia in 1948 had been necessary to forestall an American-sponsored coup.

As *Cold War* moves forward, it only rolls downhill. In a segment entitled "Reds," devoted to the 1950s, the narrator tells us in the sternest of tones that "both sides turned their fear inward against their own people. They hunted the enemy within." On the Soviet side, there was the "Gulag—the secret universe of labor camps." On the American side, there was McCarthyism, a phenomenon that saw people "imprisoned" and "their livelihoods taken away."

Charles Krauthammer has written scathingly about this episode as a blatant example of "moral equivalence," in which the murder of tens of millions is absurdly compared with the incarceration of a number of Hollywood personalities who lost their jobs or were jailed for refusing to answer questions before congressional committees. But "Reds" is also an example of the other phenomenon noted by Krauthammer, the tendency of *Cold War* to move beyond moral equivalence to "cheap anti-Americanism." In fact, the episode fosters a lie, portraying the United States in a grotesque caricature while going a considerable distance to excuse Stalin for his monstrous crimes.

In the 1950s, Kenneth Branagh tells us, "anti-Communism became the language for a new, more defiant vision of America." In no time at all, a wave of terror descended on the United States. As "persecution spread," labor organizations were "banned, radical groups indicted, [and] demonstrations broken up." Talk of the national interest was used "to justify any method of locating subversives."

At the same time that civil liberties were being extinguished in the United States, they were also being trod on in the USSR. But in Moscow's case, according to CNN, the authorities were not engaging in a "witchhunt"; they really did have legitimate reasons for alarm. The cold war, after all, had "heightened tensions and reinforced fears, not just of internal subversion but of another war." And "obsessive" and "paranoid" as Stalin may have been, he did have real enemies. Among them was the CIA, which was carrying out a radio "propaganda" campaign directed against Eastern Europe and sending "armed exiles back into the Soviet empire." In other words, the Soviet secret police had good reason to exercise "vigilance against spies and saboteurs."

The book adds important qualifications to this ludicrous whitewashing of reality—McCarthyism, it concedes, "paled in comparison to the paranoia that permeated the Soviet system"; "what in the United States was an aberration was in the Soviet world the system itself"; and many thousands perished. It then proceeds to vitiate these perfectly valid points by portraying the United States as a society in the throes of a totalitarianism every bit as benighted as that prevailing in the USSR. Thus, if the Soviet Union suffered a "Great Terror" in which neighbors denounced neighbors and children denounced parents, the United States suffered a "Great Fear" in which "neighbors were encouraged to spy on one another. Parents were asked to inform on their children, children on their parents," and only by naming names "could penitent [American] Communists purge themselves and escape further torture by the Inquisition."

In short, the United States and the USSR in the 1950s—a period, let us remember, when the Communists, having destroyed all possibility of democracy in Eastern Europe, and having conducted outright military aggression in Korea, were still trying to foment civil war and internal subversion elsewhere in the world, including in the United States, while systematically continuing to brutalize and immiserate their own people at home—were not merely morally equivalent, they were essentially identical in key respects.

By the time CNN gets to the cold war's endgame, the last of the four junctures I propose to examine, it succeeds in doing the impossible: giving credit to Moscow for terminating the conflict, and blaming Washington for attempting to extend it.

Ronald Reagan, not surprisingly, is the scoundrel of the story; in the film, and particularly in the book, he is charged with every sin. Like his predecessor Harry Truman, Reagan is described as ignorant of foreign affairs, but also as feebleminded, exhibiting his mental impairments in direct proportion to the zeal with which he adhered to his "fervent" anti-communism.

Given Reagan's "simplistic vision of an ideological crusade against Communism," it is no surprise in CNN's eyes that his defense policy should have amounted to giving the Pentagon "almost everything it wanted." This included not only the right to attempt the "nuclear decapitation" of the Soviet political and military leadership in the event of war but also a chimerical program of missile defense, the Strategic Defense Initiative (SDI) — "Star Wars" — adopted "without any analysis of the technological problems or the costs involved." Needless to say, "these hawkish plans were funded by immense budget deficits and by cutting back on domestic welfare programs."

Reagan's unrestrained military policies were made the more threatening, we learn, by being conjoined with his "aggressive pronouncements against Communism." From his belligerent rhetoric — he was actually reckless enough to call the USSR "the focus of evil in the modern world" and "the evil empire" — it became clear that he was striving "for outright victory in the cold war." In pursuit of this ambition, which, CNN suggests, put the destruction of the entire globe at the distance of a hair's breadth, the United States found itself allied with unsavory forces everywhere: a multitude of right-wing military juntas, fanatically murderous Islamic fundamentalists in Afghanistan, and even, in Cambodia, "the genocidal Khmer Rouge." These alliances, Cold War's coffee-table book instructs us, were "a direct result of Reagan's 'noble cause' of fighting Communism."

If Reagan comes across as a superficially genial but in fact quite malevolent villain, Mikhail Gorbachev is presented by CNN as a charming prince of peace. Elected unanimously — "this was the Soviet way of doing things" — Gorbachev understood the profound and hitherto concealed truth that the Soviet Union needed "to move forward." Many in the USSR "were excited by the appointment of a young, dynamic new leader" — for some, "he was a messiah coming to save them" — and Gorbachev responded to this popular enthusiasm in kind. He "regularly visited factories and colleges" and "loved to meet people."

One hardly has to credit Reagan with single-handedly liquidating the Soviet empire to recognize that Cold War presents him in full-blown caricature. A far more generous assessment of Reagan and his policies can be found in, of all places, the memoirs of Anatoly Dobrynin, the archsupporter of détente and longtime Soviet ambassador to the United States.[4] Even as he bemoans Reagan's "gross and even primitive anti-Sovietism"

---

4. In Confidence: Moscow's Ambassador to America's Six Cold-War Presidents (1995).

and confirms that the president's rhetoric and defense policies shocked the Soviet Politburo, Dobrynin acknowledges that this cut two ways.

Dobrynin, in fact, showers Reagan not only with abuse but with accolades: "Opponents and experts alike clearly underestimated him"; he "proved to be a much deeper person than he first appeared"; he "was endowed with natural instinct, flair, and optimism"; "his imagination supported big ideas like SDI"; and, finally and most significantly considering the source, "Reagan's achievements in dealing with the Soviet Union could certainly compare favorably with, and perhaps even surpass, those of Richard Nixon and Henry Kissinger."

Similarly, one hardly needs to view Gorbachev as an unreconstructed hard-liner to understand that CNN's adulatory sketch is designed primarily to depict him as the exact opposite of Reagan. (Gorbachev himself is quoted calling Reagan a "caveman" and a "dinosaur.") In addition to all his winning personal qualities, Gorbachev, we are told, also grasped the importance of "ending the arms race," going so far as to propose cutting the USSR's nuclear missile force in half if only the United States would scrap "Star Wars." Predictably, the ever-bellicose Reagan, "urged on by his hawkish national-security adviser," said no.

Gorbachev, it bears remembering, is reviled in Russia today (as he was back then, too, pace CNN), and it also bears remembering one of the reasons why. The last Soviet leader began his tenure in office not as a democrat or a reformer but as a true member of the faith, who intended to restore the ailing communist church to health through a policy of *uskoreniye*. Despite its bevy of Russian consultants and advisers, CNN's book mendaciously translates this word as "acceleration of reform," adding that "to awaken Soviet society from its lethargy, Gorbachev felt it was essential to inspire working people."

In fact, *uskoreniye* simply means "acceleration," and it was the slogan under which Gorbachev, in his first flailing efforts to wrestle with the USSR's insoluble problems, attempted to speed up the tempo at which the working people worked, not, however, by "inspiring" them but by imposing greater discipline. Unable to overcome the national torpor through such measures as a crackdown on "shopping" (i.e., standing in unending queues for basic staples) during working hours, he then abandoned this approach in favor of other tinkerings that only managed to "accelerate" the system's complete collapse.

The error in translation here is a small but telling example of the spirit of the book—if not, indeed, of the documentary as well. It goes without saying that neither Gorbachev nor Reagan was the unalloyed creature of good or evil that CNN strains to suggest. Just as there are issues worth debating about the origins of the cold war, so there are issues worth debating about its end, not least among them the question of whether the corroding Soviet superstructure collapsed in the late 1980s merely by virtue of its own deadweight or as a result of pressure brought to bear from the United States. Whatever view one takes on that point, the film, and the book even more so, employs crude rhetorical tricks to offer a burlesque not only of the motives of the actors on the Soviet side but of the undeniable risks Reagan assumed in frontally challenging the USSR at a moment when its army was on the march and, militarily, at least, it was becoming mightier by the day.

Among the troubling matters raised by this entire CNN project is the growing authority accorded to "oral history," now becoming a major subspecialty of the historical profession itself. Even if *Cold War* had truly confined itself to doing what Gaddis says it set out to do—namely, allowing "all kinds of people simply to tell their stories," without attempting to settle issues of historical responsibility—there would still be ample reasons to object to it.

History, as Gaddis is well aware, is not just a random assemblage of "stories," all equally interesting and equally authoritative. The raw materials of history need precisely the sort of sifting and weighing that competent historians are trained to undertake; they require, at the very least, evaluation, the same task a jury performs in a court of law to determine whether testimony is credible or self-serving and deceptive. And after that evaluation is performed, those materials need to be placed into some larger framework or context. Despite what Gaddis has written in the *New York Times*, the mere fact that *Cold War* shows us pictures of various Soviet atrocities is utterly irrelevant to the charge that it systematically portrays the United States and the USSR as moral equivalents.

By emphasizing "minimal narration" and an "international perspective," and by excluding interviews with professional historians and focusing only on "participants in the events," *Cold War* was destined from the start to be, at best, an exercise in historical distortion. A parade of silver-haired former Soviet apparatchiks appears on screen, wearing elegant suits and looking every bit like American academics as they tell us in soothing tones what may be truths or what may be lies. The former KGB chief Vladimir Kryuchkov, invited to explain how the USSR sent its army across an international frontier in 1979, generously complies: "If we didn't go into Afghanistan, then some other countries would." Perhaps Kryuchkov is here accurately restating the considerations of the Soviet Politburo in the fall and winter of that year. Perhaps, throughout a long career swimming inside the entrails of the Soviet Union's secret police, he was always a scrupulous truth teller. Or perhaps not. Whatever the case, viewers of *Cold War* are never made aware of the enormous question mark that dangles over the words of such a man, a torturer whose recollections are here given equal weight with the recollections of the tortured.[5]

Still, in the end, it is not its failure properly to evaluate the numerous interviews from which it is woven that is the most objectionable aspect of *Cold War*. It is the absurd evaluations the program does provide, both in the accompanying book and in the tendentious commentary of the narrator. And that, too, raises a question: Why is it that so many people in the West continue to cling to a version of history in which the most egregious Soviet conduct is excused or explained away, while the United States is condemned for transgressions it did not commit?

In the 1930s, according to CNN's book, those in the West who cast their sympathies with the USSR did so because they "hated the inequalities and injustices they saw in their own societies." In addition, they were "unaware" of what was going on in the Soviet Union, a country that was "a closed book." This explanation is itself a falsehood.

Despite the hermetic seal Stalin attempted to impose throughout his

---

5. In the segments of *Cold War* devoted to Soviet-American competition in the Third World, the communist side is consistently represented by attractive-looking, articulate spokesmen—Soviets, Cubans, Nicaraguans, and Angolans—who passionately and persuasively defend their cause. The U.S. side, by contrast, is represented by a gaggle of cynical ex-CIA men who not only look like thugs from central casting but speak like them as well. By this means is a process that looks like evenhandedness put in the service of deliberate historical falsification.

dictatorial reign, there was no shortage in the West of English-language reporting making it plain that a man-made calamity was unfolding in the Soviet Union. The "idealists" (CNN's term) who in the 1930s regarded the USSR as a progressive beacon for humanity were not unaware of what was going on; they fully understood, as Lenin liked to repeat, that, when you chop wood, the chips will fly. But when it came to those chips—millions of innocent people being done to death by starvation or pistol shots to the back of the head—they consciously averted their eyes.

Today, after the publication of Aleksandr Solzhenitsyn's *The Gulag Archipelago*, after the opening of Soviet archives themselves, after the accumulation of so many unalterable facts, it is no longer possible to claim one is "unaware" of what the Soviet Union was and how it behaved over the course of its disastrous seven decades. That behavior fully merits Reagan's accurate term for it: "the focus of evil in the modern world." Yet, as the very existence of the CNN documentary testifies, the same impulse to avert one's eyes and the same hatred of democratic society are with us still. It beggars the imagination that John Lewis Gaddis, a historian who has shown he knows better, should have lent his name to such an exercise.

Second only to the rampage that Hitler embarked on in Europe in 1939, the cold war was a terrible conflict in the terrible century that is now drawing to its close. As younger generations that did not live through those terrors come of age, CNN's twenty-four-part *Cold War* series, with its panoply of educational appurtenances, is likely to be the one version of this momentous stretch of the past that most people will see and remember. Though the film succeeds, sometimes brilliantly, at giving a vivid sense of what kinds of tribulations and anguish and nightmares the Soviet-American conflict entailed, it nevertheless advances an utterly false explanation of what the struggle was all about.

Although it remains unfashionable to say so plainly, Harry Truman and Ronald Reagan had it right: At bottom the cold war was a colossal battle between good and evil, between freedom and slavery, between democracy and totalitarianism. It was also a battle in which, at every step of the way, tremendously difficult moral choices had to be faced by the forces of good. On some occasions those forces, led by the United States, took actions that were questionable, even highly questionable; on some rare occasions, they took actions that were indefensible and wrong.

But recognizing the moral ambiguities of the war, and the occasional but very real moral shortcomings and failures of the West, is one thing; CNN's version of history is entirely another. As that version proceeds, the "noble cause" of defending freedom is mocked, good is turned into evil and evil into good, and the moral and political categories that distinguish a democratic country like the United States from a totalitarian one like the USSR are blurred and then entirely erased. Considering the great lengths to which the Soviet Union went to falsify history, the fact that *Cold War* is today being introduced into the standard curriculum of American high schools is a nightmarish irony. It is also an insult to all those who paid a terrible price for risking their own freedom in freedom's name.

Letters

TO THE EDITOR:

> *My good blade carves the casques of men;*
> *My stout lance thrusteth sure.*
> *My strength is as the strength of ten,*
> *Because my heart is pure.*

Arise Sir Gabriel Schoenfeld, the Galahad of our day, as well as the Don Quixote—tilting at windmills. I have tried to take seriously his piece "Twenty-four Lies about the Cold War." But I am not sure, even as I sit down to write, that I can do it. I once knew a television series of the sort he commends to your readers in which the witnesses and the narrator combined with the protagonist to assure viewers that he had acted nobly at all times and deserved only our admiration. It was called *Mountbatten.* I once asked Lord Louis Mountbatten if ever in his life he had made a mistake—he answered, "No." Later, in an interview for the television series *The World at War*, he suggested I have him introduced by an acolyte who would say what he wanted said in his praise before he spoke. I declined; the three-cheers-for-us school of history suffered a setback and should not, in my view, be resurrected, especially not for the cold war.

Mr. Schoenfeld begins, beguilingly, by praising the *Cold War* series for the depth of its research and the skill of its compilation, recognized by a Peabody Award in the United States and by a BAFTA nomination in the United Kingdom. But he attacks the series as history; Mr. Schoenfeld would have written it differently. Of course. I write now not principally to quarrel with that—though I may—but to set the record straight on key facts.

First, as John Lewis Gaddis has pointed out, editorial responsibility for the series is with me and with my co–executive producer, Pat Mitchell, president of CNN Productions. John Lewis Gaddis, like Vladislav Zubok and Professor Lawrence Freedman, head of the department of war studies at King's College, London, acted as consultants to the series. They are not responsible for its content; Pat Mitchell and I are.

Second, although John Lewis Gaddis was good enough to read the typescript of the book, written by Taylor Downing and by me, that accompanies the series, he is in no way responsible for what it contains. Mr. Gaddis will be judged by his peers as the preeminent U.S. historian of the cold war because of his own reflective and authoritative volumes. Nor is CNN in any way responsible for the book, except that the series Ted Turner commissioned sparked it off. What CNN is responsible for is an imaginative *Cold War* web site, offering a critical apparatus to complement the series. It has had more than twelve million visits so far.

I note that Mr. Schoenfeld is senior editor of *Commentary*, which hurts, for I always had the idea that *Commentary* was a serious journal. He quotes selectively and willfully or inadvertently—I know which is worse— misunderstands and misrepresents. I take only one example: the extent of Leninist/Stalinist terror, which he thinks is seriously understated in both documentary and book. It is true there is not much about Lenin in a narrative whose effective starting point is 1945. But here is the book, pages 8 and 9:

> In 1937 the terror extended into almost every walk of life. Artists and writers, scientists and doctors, were executed or imprisoned. Top generals in the army were purged, and one in three of the entire officer corps were arrested. Millions of ordinary peasants and workers were also denounced as "enemies of the people." A knock on the door in the night, exile to a forced labor camp, a bullet in the back of the head, became the hallmarks of Stalin's rule. George Kennan, gazing out of his office window above Red Square, thought to himself that he was looking out over "one of the bloodiest spots in the world." Stalin sent between 17 million and 22 million of his own countrymen to their deaths during the 1930's, including those who starved or died of maltreatment in the labor camps of Siberia—nearly three times the number of victims that would be claimed by Hitler's Holocaust.

Here's the documentary, episode one: "Stalin was master of the economic plan. But he was also a tyrant who tolerated no failure and no
criticism. . . . Privately owned fields became collectivized prairies. The
cost of collectivization was the murder of millions of peasants and renewed
famine. The truth was kept secret." On which a Soviet citizen comments:
"People didn't know about the bad things. All the achievements were put
down to [Stalin's] initiatives. Those who knew otherwise would shut up.
They knew if they said anything, they would be imprisoned and shot. It
was a regime of terror."

And in episode six, "Reds"—which deliberately compares and contrasts McCarthyite hysteria, which claimed two lives (the Rosenbergs,
convicted and guilty of espionage), with Stalin's millions of victims—
Susanna Pechuro, a student whose comrades were executed but who
herself survived the Gulag, testifies:

> There are some things that are so awful I don't let myself remember
> them, because if I do I can't sleep for weeks. They pulled children out
> of the arms of their screaming mothers, and then beat the mothers. The
> children just disappeared, they never knew what happened to them
> afterward. There was nothing more awful than that, even though I saw
> them killing people, anything else they felt like doing.

And here's the book:

> The cold war, and the reverses the nation faced, generated in the United
> States what has been called the Great Fear. The Soviet Union endured
> far worse: the Great Terror. McCarthyism, and every other American
> hysteria, paled in comparison to the paranoia that permeated the Soviet
> system and Communist East Europe in the late 1940s and early 1950s,
> as it had done during Stalin's reign of terror in the 1930s. Hundreds of
> thousands of people were sent to labor camps. Many thousands, loyal
> party members, were executed. In Hungary as many as one family in
> three had a member in jail during the Stalinist period. In the Soviet
> Union and Eastern Europe, conformity was everything. No dissent was
> allowed; independent thought was fiercely tracked down, rooted out, and
> repressed. What in the United States was an aberration was in the Soviet
> world the system itself.

How can Mr. Schoenfeld claim that I and my colleagues treat the two cold war great powers as moral equals? He can only do so by ignoring plain evidence to the contrary. His case is built on sand; to refute it, I have only to invite your readers to watch the series and read the book.

It is certainly true, though, that the series is less judgmental and more evenhanded than Mr. Schoenfeld might welcome. So is all good history. The world does not easily divide into goodies and baddies as children's games, ancient Hollywood myths, and now *Commentary* would have it. And we can learn from both sides. Nazis contributed to *The World at War* and made it richer and more complex. It is obviously right that Soviet eyewitnesses should participate in *Cold War* and indeed Poles, Czechoslovaks, Hungarians, Germans who bore its brunt and paid its price.

The cold war, particularly at its outset, was both an ideological conflict and an exercise in realpolitik. Truman, Eisenhower, Kennedy, Johnson, Nixon, Carter, Reagan, and Bush come out of it as major, serious, even heroic players on the world stage. I defy anyone to view the series in its entirety and not feel the strong continuity in U.S. foreign policy that first acted to contain communism and then saw it crumble into surrender and defeat. But these were humans, not gods. Does anyone doubt that Harry Truman grew in the presidency? Or that Ronald Reagan surprised us, in the alacrity with which he reached for agreement on arms limitation with an "evil empire"? But both Truman and Reagan, in their own utterances, and in the words of those who worked with them, are depicted at full stature in *Cold War*.

Mr. Schoenfeld's farrago of imaginings gave me two particular pleasures. He cites, feelingly, the ghastly description of the death of Peter Fechter at the Berlin Wall—the East unwilling, the West thinking itself unable to save him. I agree with him; this moves and chills us. Charles Krauthammer, in the *Washington Post*, however, took the very same sequence as an indefensible instance of our attributing "moral equivalence" to both sides' responsibility for Fechter's death.

And in a footnote that belongs in a comic book, Mr. Schoenfeld charges:

> In the segments of *Cold War* devoted to the Soviet-American competition in the Third World, the communist side is consistently represented by

attractive-looking, articulate spokesmen—Soviets, Cubans, Nicaraguans, and Angolans—who passionately and persuasively defend their cause. The U.S. side, by contrast, is represented by a gaggle of cynical ex-CIA men who not only look like thugs from central casting but speak like them as well. By this means is a process that looks like evenhandedness put in the service of deliberate historical falsification.

If we include Afghanistan in the Third World, and also the film's episode on spies, this fanciful paragraph is a slur on noted public servants, all CIA: John Stockwell, Howard Hunt, Paul Wimert, Duane Claridge, Frank Anderson, Dr. Charles Cogan, David Murphy, Melvin Goodman, Sydney Graybeal, Joe Bulik, Admiral Stansfield Turner, Jeanne Verte-feuille, and Sandy Grimes, among others. I will take them against the KGB any day; they came not from central casting but from the real world.

More seriously, Mr. Schoenfeld's careless charge of "deliberate historical falsification" is totally unsubstantiated. It is a particular travesty that *Commentary* should have given his piece the title "Twenty-four Lies about the Cold War" since he signally fails to indict book or series for even one. (There is an erratum in the book, by the way. I offer a bottle of fine Scotch malt to the first *Commentary* reader to spot it and let me know.)

The last word belongs, Mr. Schoenfeld suggests, "to those who paid a terrible price for risking their own freedom in freedom's name." In the series, I award it to Vaclav Havel: "Communism as a system went against life, against man's fundamental needs; against the need for freedom; the need to be enterprising, to associate freely; against the will of the nation. It suppressed national identity. Something that goes against life may last a long time—but sooner or later, it will collapse." And I rest my case.

JEREMY ISAACS
Jeremy Isaacs Productions Ltd.
London, UK

TO THE EDITOR:

In his long, occasionally thoughtful, but ultimately harsh essay on CNN's *Cold War*, Gabriel Schoenfeld wonders why the series does not in all respects reflect the perspective of my recent book, *We Now Know: Rethinking Cold War History*, which he has generously reviewed. The answer is simple. I authored the book. I consulted on the television series and, to a lesser extent, the printed materials associated with it. I did not, in any part of the CNN project, have editorial control.

There are, of course, some things I would have done differently had I had such authority. But should I have withdrawn from the series because I did not get my way at all times? It never occurred to me to do so, for several reasons. First, the ground rules were clear from the outset: The producers, not the consultants, were to have the last word. Second, I had assumed—naively, it now seems—that critics would understand the distinction between authorship and consultancy. Finally, I remain convinced that this series presents the cold war more effectively than has been done or ever will be done again on television. I am proud to have my name associated with it—as a consultant.

JOHN LEWIS GADDIS
Yale University
New Haven, Connecticut

TO THE EDITOR:

Gabriel Schoenfeld claims that CNN's *Cold War* is an anti-American concoction that excuses "the most egregious Soviet conduct" and ignores a battle "between good and evil, between freedom and slavery, between democracy and totalitarianism." He also claims that some episodes contain "deliberate historical falsification."

I feel conflicted by these charges. As a Russian who very much longed for freedom and democracy, I am with Mr. Schoenfeld. But as a historian and one of the principal consultants for the series, I simply do not see anti-American "conspiracy" or falsification in the film.

I believe that Mr. Schoenfeld has many axes to grind: against the communist sympathizers and fellow travelers of the 1930s, "revisionist" historians of the 1960s, prodétente liberals of the 1970s, and Ted Turner and "peaceniks" of the 1980s. This ideological bent may explain why he approaches the cold war not as a complex historical drama with multiple meanings and experiences but simply as a crusade against the "evil empire."

Mr. Schoenfeld is not satisfied with damning the series with faint praise. Instead, he "unmasks" a hostile pattern using selective quotations and his own flawed judgment of history. He ignores *Cold War*'s praise for

Western policies of opposition to Stalinism in Europe (see the programs "Berlin Blockade" and "Marshall Plan") and in Asia ("Korea"). But he castigates the series for demonstrating that an exaggerated American perception of the communist threat contributed to a dangerous nuclear arms race, as well as insecurity and some antidemocratic practices at home.

I agree with Mr. Schoenfeld that *Cold War* should have highlighted more the massive Soviet penetration of the United States before and during World War II. However, as Allen Weinstein and Alexander Vassilyev reveal in their new book, *The Haunted Wood*, as of November 1945 (i.e., before the cold war began), the Soviet "fifth column" in the United States was compromised by defections and quickly melted away.

As one responsible for facts (if not all the judgments) in CNN's *Cold War*, I categorically reject Mr. Schoenfeld's claim that the series drew a "moral equivalence" between Stalin's empire and the United States. The series recapitulates the horrors of the Stalinist regime, and, with footage of the concentration camps at Kolyma, it shows graphically the evil of the communist system. I disagree equally with those left-radical historians who claim that *Cold War* blames Stalin exclusively for the origins of the cold war and defends most U.S. policies. Both sides, I believe, build a straw man from the series and use it to advocate their agendas.

CNN's *Cold War* tries to convey to the audience the moral ambiguity so often found in history and the complexity of human personalities. It presents Ronald Reagan, for instance, as both a contributor to war danger and a partner to Gorbachev in ending the cold war. But for Mr. Schoenfeld, everyone is either a hero or a villain: Reagan is without blemish and beyond reproach.

CNN's *Cold War* is not without flaws and biases. But its main thrust, from "The Iron Curtain" to "The Wall Falls Down," does not hide the obvious fact that freedom was on one side and oppression and tyranny on the other. Sometimes the series is critical of American actions. But should American foreign policy escape critical judgment just because the other side was incomparably worse? U.S. alliances and deals with Mao Tse-tung, the apartheid regime in South Africa, and dictators here and there may have been validated by the victory over communism. But not everyone around the world would agree.

In the great Western tradition of free critical discourse, the series presents many viewpoints and experiences. For me, as a former subject of the "evil empire," this tradition was the most obvious victor in CNN's *Cold War*.

VLADISLAV M. ZUBOK
National Security Archive
George Washington University
Washington, D.C.

TO THE EDITOR:

Gabriel Schoenfeld's "Twenty-four Lies about the Cold War" is an especially acute, balanced, and probing account of the CNN version of Soviet-American relations. In a cultural environment in which the writing of history has been superseded in part by the televising of ideology as history, such a statement becomes necessary and not just welcome. Thumbs up for Mr. Schoenfeld's razor-sharp critique.

IRVING LOUIS HOROWITZ
Rutgers University
New Brunswick, New Jersey

TO THE EDITOR:

I read Gabriel Schoenfeld's article on CNN's cold war lies with great interest. It is amazing what TV will do—great technical virtuosity combined with mindlessness.

The series is not, however, the only example of how historians have let their biases affect their narratives. Recently Thomas Cargill and I looked at the way high school history textbooks treat the Great Depression and found that the discussion was strongly biased and totally out of line with modern scholarship. I wonder in how many other cases popularizations by historians are spreading misinformation.

THOMAS MAYER
University of California
Davis, California

TO THE EDITOR:

Gabriel Schoenfeld admirably illuminates some of the moral fog that envelops CNN's *Cold War* series. He might have reflected more, however, on the most disturbing aspect of *Cold War*, which was not its startling relativism or even the undue respect (and airtime) it gave to the likes of Fidel Castro.

What is most unsettling and irresponsible about the series is the Orwellian way it uses language both to reorder history and to protect Soviet leaders from too harsh a judgment of their actions. The narrative is not merely relativistic; it actually misdirects the audience.

Take, for example, the depiction of the reigniting of the cold war in the early 1980s. We are shown the following sequence of events: Reagan's "evil empire" speech, his speech announcing the Strategic Defense Initiative, Yuri Andropov's accession to the Soviet leadership, and a worldwide nuclear war warning by the KGB. The implication is clear to the average viewer: Reagan came to power and made outrageous speeches, scared the Soviets silly, and nearly started World War III.

The problem is that these events did not happen even remotely in this order. The KGB war warning was put in place in 1981 under Brezhnev; Andropov came to power a year later; and Reagan's speeches were a year after that. The idea that Reagan was responding to, rather than causing, Soviet actions is not likely to occur to anyone listening to *Cold War*'s narrative because, in CNN's version of events, such an interpretation is logically impossible.

Likewise, arms reduction talks in Geneva in 1983 were not "broken off," nor did Soviet tanks in Lithuania just "attack" in 1991. The Soviets walked out of the negotiations, and someone ordered those tanks to attack. But rather than raise the disturbing question of who sent in the tanks — the series makes plain that Mikhail Gorbachev ended the cold war, so it could not have been him — the script simply phrases the event indirectly and moves on.

This is more disturbing than the revisionism, bias, and overemphasis on the recollections of torturers and dictators that Mr. Schoenfeld rightly decries. John Lewis Gaddis claims that his students would find "laughable" the assertion that the CNN series is guilty of moral relativism. Of course they would. For students, or ordinary viewers, to decide whether the show is really arguing the case for moral relativism would have required *Cold*

War to make that case explicitly instead of burying it in obfuscatory language and a garbled retelling of events. This is not, as *Cold War*'s producers claim, history told in anecdotes. It is history written in Newspeak.

THOMAS M. NICHOLS
U.S. Naval War College
Newport, Rhode Island

(The views expressed here are those of the author only and not the United States government.)

TO THE EDITOR:

Gabriel Schoenfeld's analysis of CNN's *Cold War* raises profound issues about the difficulties of teaching American history from an international perspective — difficulties that Americans like me, who teach in overseas universities, must confront daily.

Mr. Schoenfeld asks, "Why is it that so many people in the West continue to cling to a version of history in which the most egregious Soviet conduct is excused or explained away, while the United States is condemned for transgressions it did not commit?" I am not sure this question is fairly phrased, but it is true that, when considering the cold war, many people in the West hold the United States to a higher standard than they do the Soviet Union. We expect political murder and repression of freedom from the Soviets. When their leaders rise above these practices, they deserve our surprise, if not our praise.

On the other hand, we expect the United States to uphold the civil liberties that are the foundation of our Constitution — for without them it cannot be the "good" in the "colossal battle between good and evil" that Mr. Schoenfeld describes. And when it falls short of these expectations, it deserves our criticism.

American excesses of enthusiasm in the prosecution of the cold war both at home and abroad have hampered Americans' ability to assert unflinchingly our national virtue. If we wish credibly to point to the basic American commitment to civil freedoms, we must also acknowledge that we ourselves have threatened the integrity of this commitment.

ERIC RAUCHWAY
Mansfield College, Oxford University
Oxford, England

TO THE EDITOR:

I salute Gabriel Schoenfeld for his eloquent account of the flaws in CNN's *Cold War*. His article raises the question of competition: Why is there not a visually appealing account of the cold war written by the "good guys"? Somewhere out there right now, someone has the talent to execute such a project. And, surely, there is another someone out there who is rich enough to fund it. If the truth is to win out, some of us had better get into the popular culture battle or we will leave the field to CNN and others whose agenda does not serve the truth.

RUSSELL ROBERTS
Washington University
St. Louis, Missouri

TO THE EDITOR:

"Twenty-four Lies about the Cold War" was enlightening, but I wonder whether a different title might have helped readers grasp the theme more easily. Gabriel Schoenfeld's essential point is that the CNN series commits the revisionist mistake of seeing the adversaries in the cold war as morally equivalent. Perhaps Mr. Schoenfeld might have called the article, as he writes on his last page, "Truman and Reagan Had It Right, the Soviet Union Was an Evil Empire."

Congratulations on a splendid article.

JACKSON TOBY
Rutgers University
New Brunswick, New Jersey

Response

Gabriel Schoenfeld

CNN's promotional material boasts that John Lewis Gaddis and Vladislav Zubok "commented on every outline, every rough-cut, every final script" in order to keep the documentary to the "ascertainable truth." Among the historical advisers, Mr. Gaddis read "every word" of the book accompanying the show.

Mr. Gaddis now states that he only "consulted on the television series and, to a lesser extent, the printed materials associated with it." He did not, he avers, "have editorial control" of any part of the project. Although there are some things he "would have done differently," he declines to spell out what they are.

It would have been most interesting to learn precisely what Mr. Gaddis would have done differently and why. Certainly, in the article he wrote about the series for the "Ideas" page of the *New York Times* earlier this year (January 9, 1999), one finds no trace of the unspecified reservations he now claims to entertain. To judge by that article and his present reticence, he appears to be a very faithful "consultant."

Given the huge discrepancy between Mr. Gaddis's own evolving views as set forth in his published works and the revisionist line taken in the CNN film and book, my own hunch is that the network's publicists and producers were more interested in capitalizing on Mr. Gaddis's sterling reputation as a scholar than on his sterling scholarly judgment. Why he allowed his good name to be associated with such a scandalous product I cannot say. I find myself mildly heartened that he now disclaims responsibility for the *Cold War* series. At the same time, I am profoundly disheartened that a Yale professor would say he is "proud" to be associated with a product that negates his own best work. Or perhaps, as Mr. Gaddis suggests, I have "naively" misunderstood all the subtle distinctions involved in the consulting business.

Vladislav Zubok begins his letter promisingly by stating that as a freedom- and democracy-loving Russian, he is "with" me. But then, evidently donning his consultant's hat, he proceeds to express reservations about the "many axes" I grind against "peaceniks," revisionist historians, Ted Turner, and the like. In particular, he disputes the idea that there was an anti-American "conspiracy" in the way the film came to be produced.

This criticism is baffling. Though I speak of an anti-American mindset, the word *conspiracy* does not appear in my article at all, and I am mystified by Mr. Zubok's motive in attributing it to me. But, then, no less mystifying is his eagerness to concur with me on another matter—namely, "that *Cold War* should have highlighted more the massive Soviet penetration of the United States before and during World War II." While I welcome his solidarity, he is agreeing with me on a point I never made or even touched upon.

That so careless a reader and writer served CNN as one "responsible for facts (if not all the judgments)" leaves me with a better understanding of the origins of at least some of the documentary's numerous foibles and flaws.

Sir Jeremy Isaacs's resourceful letter is another kettle of fish entirely, complete with piranhas. It is, I admit, a kind of honor to be poked at as "the Galahad of our day" or even a "Don Quixote" by so worthy a British knight. And it is also a relief to find here no easy attempt to escape censure with the excuse that one was merely serving as Ted Turner's hired horseman.

To begin with, Sir Jeremy suggests (in words echoed by Vladislav Zubok) that mine is a simpleminded version of history, in which a perfectly virtuous West triumphs over a thoroughly iniquitous East. The world, he corrects me, "does not easily divide into goodies and baddies as children's games, ancient Hollywood myths, and now *Commentary* would have it."

The form of humor employed here has a name: It is called caricature, and it fails to meet my argument. In my article I took special cognizance of what I called the "moral ambiguities of the cold war." On some occasions, I wrote, the United States and its allies "took actions that were questionable, even highly questionable; on some, rare occasions, they took actions that were indefensible and wrong." Does this sound like a conception of a world composed solely of "goodies and baddies"?

But it is one thing to recognize shades of gray in what was a great moral contest. It is another thing entirely to blur the distinction between black and white or even attempt to erase it entirely, as the CNN documentary does throughout. Consider in this context the question of Soviet terror. Although *tu quoque* is not an argument, the fact is that Sir Jeremy is himself baldly misrepresenting when he alleges that I misrepresent both documentary and book. Citing a number of extremely vivid passages that accurately characterize the scale and scope of the Soviet nightmare, he then complains, "How can Mr. Schoenfeld claim that I and my colleagues treat the two cold war great powers as moral equals?" The answer is very simple.

Contrary to Sir Jeremy's letter, I never said that the extent of Stalin's terror (Lenin's terror is something else) was "seriously understated in documentary and book"—in fact, I offer him a bottle of the finest Siberian vodka (distilled from prerevolutionary potatoes) if he can document otherwise. Indeed, I specifically cited some of the very passages from the book that Sir Jeremy now asserts I ignored ("the Soviet Union endured far worse"; "McCarthyism, and every other American hysteria, paled in comparison to the paranoia that permeated the Soviet system"), singling them out as "perfectly valid points." I then proceeded to show how these perfectly valid points are vitiated by the portrayal of America as a society in the throes of its own homegrown version of totalitarianism.

In this portrayal, both film and book apply Soviet-style words and phrases to the United States: "torture," "persecution," "purge," "inquisition," and, finally, "Great Fear"—a fear in which "neighbors were encouraged to spy on one another. Parents were asked to inform on their children, children on their parents," etc. It was on the basis of (among many other things) this terminologically loaded comparison of the Stalin and McCarthy periods that I found Sir Jeremy's documentary guilty of treating "the two cold war great powers as moral equals."

Nor is this the only issue Sir Jeremy dodges, whether willfully or inadvertently (I too know which is worse). Consider the project's version of the founder of Soviet communism, Vladimir Ilych Lenin. My charge was hardly, as Sir Jeremy summarizes it, that "there is not much" about Lenin. On the contrary, I would contend that too much was said about Lenin in both documentary and book, including passages in which Sir Jeremy describes the Soviet dictator's "deep commitment to bettering the lives of ordinary Russians" or declares that Lenin's "socialist principles were meant to ensure decent education, free health care, common ownership of land, and fairness for all." To anyone remotely familiar with Lenin's bloody thoughts and deeds, it is not difficult to see why Sir Jeremy should shun mention of these indefensibly pink passages.

Sir Jeremy also accuses me of slurring a whole battalion of CIA officers. I thought it was clear that, in characterizing the American side as represented by a gaggle of ex-CIA thugs, I was referring only to the film's episode on Angola and Latin America. In the other episodes he tosses in—those devoted to Afghanistan and to espionage—very different sorts of problems arise. The idea, for example, that the USSR entered Afghanistan in 1979 only to keep other countries out (i.e., that it was acting "defensively") is the dominant thrust of show and book alike; it is also an interpretation so highly questionable as to border on outright falsehood. But as with many other points I raised and discussed, Sir Jeremy prefers here to tilt at a windmill of his own design.

Finally, Sir Jeremy calls the title of my article, "Twenty-four Lies about the Cold War," a "travesty" because I "signally fail to indict book or series for even one" lie. But if his hagiographic treatment of Lenin is not a lie, a "deliberate historical falsification," and itself a travesty, what is? Another lie (or perhaps two in one) is the documentary's portrayal of the cold war in Angola and Latin America. Yet another is its rendition of the Soviet invasion of Afghanistan. Thomas Nichols's letter brings to our attention a couple of more subtle but equally damning fabrications (as well as some lesser sins) that had escaped my notice. Given the space, I could easily arrive at or exceed the total of twenty-four lies specified in my article's title—one for each hour-long episode of the show.

In addition to Professor Nichols, I thank Eric Rauchway, Irving Louis Horowitz, Thomas Mayer, Russell Roberts, and Jackson Toby for their kind words. I also sincerely thank my very talented critics. I have read and admired many of John Lewis Gaddis's articles and books, and Sir Jeremy Isaacs's *The World at War* is a classic documentary that will never be surpassed. The riveting visual imagery and the stirring music and narration of *Cold War* once again demonstrate his formidable powers. All the more pity that it is such a profoundly flawed work, on so profoundly important a subject.

■   ■   ■

In a letter to the Hoover Institution Press regarding his essay on page 115 and his letter on page 20, Sir Jeremy Isaacs offered the following comments, which did not appear in *Commentary*.

Where I come from the defendant gets the last word; I shall be brief.

I challenged Mr. Schoenfeld to come up with specifics to justify his rash and outrageous charge of "24 Lies about the Cold War." He fails to produce one. A series that begins in 1945 has neither space nor obligation even to summarize Lenin's career. If Mr. Schoenfeld, reading our explicit description of Stalin's crimes—which he chose and chooses still to ignore—cannot envisage what we might have said of Lenin, that is his problem. It is not a "lie" about the cold war.

Nor are his assertions that I lie about Angola, Nicaragua, or Afghanistan any more than assertions. In not one instance does he bring home a specific allegation of falsehood, detail even an error of fact. Twenty-four charges, and not one that sticks. *Parturiunt montes; nascitur ridiculus mus.* I prefer my caricature to his calumny. If he will stop telling lies about me, I will stop telling the truth about him.

2

The Cold War, Television, and the Approximation of Truth

John Lewis Gaddis

John Lewis Gaddis is the Robert A. Lovett Professor of History at Yale University. He is the author, most recently, of *We Now Know: Rethinking Cold War History*, and served as a historical consultant for CNN's *Cold War*.

I take it as a given that we can never know the truth, the whole truth, and nothing but the truth about anything that happened in the past. It's tough enough to make sense of what we, as individuals, directly experience in the present. When we expand the inquiry to what others before us have experienced—especially when the "others" in question are entire societies and when the "past" extends beyond what any living person can remember—then the search for truth becomes all the more difficult. We can't rerun history in the way that we can repeat experiments in chemistry or physics to confirm that we've got it right. We're stuck with what remains of the past, and with what we ourselves make of what remains. And that is a tenuous basis indeed for getting at the truth.

Yet I also take it as a given that dinosaurs once walked the earth. No human being ever saw, heard, or was eaten by any of these creatures; but no one today would classify dinosaurs, alongside dragons, as mythical beasts. The reason is that the remains of dinosaurs exist, from which we can extract enough information to command a consensus among the experts—and among small children—that they were real. This doesn't extend to all details: Much is still disputed, much may never be known. But there is sufficient "truth" here to set dinosaurs apart from dragons, and thus to acknowledge the place in the past they occupied.

I take it as a given, as well, that we can never know the exact dimensions of even the most accessible physical landscape. Just how far is it, for example, from New York to New Haven? It depends: Are the measurements to be made in miles, meters, or microns? The answers will vary in each case because the smaller the scale the more detail each measurement will pick up. There is, strictly speaking, no "true" answer to this question.[1] And yet, people find their way between New York and New Haven all the time, with no greater difficulty than the occasional traffic jam or commuter train tie-up.

Finally, I take it as a given that physicists do not know, and may never know, whether light is a particle or a wave. Their failure to settle this most fundamental of issues did not stop them, though, from building an atomic bomb. They simply agreed, on this point, to disagree and to get on with the task at hand, thereby demonstrating in the most dramatic manner imaginable that the achievement of "truth" is not in all instances a prerequisite for effective action.

What these examples show is that *approximations* of truth suffice for paleontologists, cartographers, and physicists. They carry on quite well in the absence of absolutes. They refuse to let their inability to agree on everything paralyze them. They understand the complexity of reality, the inadequacies of the capabilities with which we can observe it, and the conclusion that necessarily follows: that if we had to *replicate* the world in which we live before attempting to comprehend it, we would never get anywhere. We compromise by *representing* reality, whether in the form of a *Brontosaurus* model in a museum, a map of southern Connecticut, or the blueprints for building a nuclear warhead. We approach the truth, but we never quite get there. And yet, we manage pretty well.

Historians function in much the same way. Like paleontologists, they represent events and environments they can never themselves experience; but they do not simply imagine these, as an artist or a novelist might do. They must fit their representations to surviving archives, artifacts, and memories—the historian's equivalent of the fossil record. Like cartographers, historians present their findings in forms accessible to those who will use them. A "complete" history of anything would be as impractical as a totally accurate map of Bridgeport, which would of course have to be the same size, shape, and texture as Bridgeport. Like physicists, historians agree to disagree even on very fundamental issues—and yet they do so, most of the time at least, with respect for opposing points of view, and with

1. See, on this point, James Gleick, *Chaos: Making a New Science* (New York: Viking, 1987), pp. 94–96.

a determination to get on with the task at hand. For they know that even "truths" as self-evident as a Newtonian clockwork universe can, in time, be overthrown.

Cold war historians have seen many apparent "truths" overthrown. "Orthodox" scholars insisted, during the 1950s and the early 1960s, that the Soviet Union had been solely responsible for that conflict. "Revisionists" reversed that interpretation over the next decade, holding the United States chiefly to blame. "Postrevisionists" then tried to find a middle ground between these extremes, with only limited success. Despite such striking differences, all of these interpretations of cold war history had two things in common: Their advocates did not know the outcome of the event they were attempting to chronicle, and—because Soviet, East European, and Chinese sources were closed to them—they had access to the archival record of only one side. They were writing history from within their subject, rather as if Jonah had attempted to characterize the whale that swallowed him from the limited perspective of its gullet.

By the end of the 1980s, though, the Soviet Union was going belly-up, the cold war was winding down, and historians could begin to see, for the first time, the possibility of representing that subject in the way that most history is represented: with knowledge of how it all came out, and with access to the archives—and the memories—of all the major participants. There arose during the early 1990s, as a consequence, a "new" cold war history that was, in its relationship to the "old," something like what Einstein had been to Newton. Everything required reconsideration, and the conclusions that followed—which even now are highly preliminary—were bound to be controversial.

The "truth" about the cold war, therefore, has shifted with time. Even today no one can claim to have pinned it down without starting an argument. The subject looms too large in the consciousness of those who lived through it to allow the detachment that is possible for the more distant past. The historians are nowhere near agreement on how to represent it. *Any* television documentary on the cold war, therefore, would have had the critics ready to pounce.

When the word got out, though, that Ted Turner had conceived, financed, and—at least in the United States—would be broadcasting a new cold war documentary, the fur really began to fly. Turner is not exactly known for shyness. He expresses his views openly, frequently, and at times imprudently. The possibility that the "Mouth of the South" might use his particular representation of cold war history, not just as a mouthpiece but as a loud and obnoxious trumpet, set all kinds of alarm bells ringing.[2]

I myself worried about this when I was asked to serve as a historical consultant on the project. It was reassuring to learn, however, that Turner had asked Sir Jeremy Isaacs, whose classic World War II documentary, *World at War*, set the standard for the responsible portrayal of history on television, to produce the series. I was also relieved to hear that Turner had requested of Isaacs only two things: that *Cold War* tell its story from an international, not just an American perspective, and that its tone not be triumphalist. These guidelines posed no problems for me or for my British and Russian colleagues, Lawrence Freedman and Vladislav Zubok; we would have insisted on them even if Turner had not.

For with the availability of new Soviet, East European, and Chinese sources, our fellow cold war historians would never have taken the series seriously had it sought only to perpetuate an Americocentric view. Avoiding triumphalism also made sense because self-congratulatory history is rarely very good history: Winners as well as losers have their shortcomings and need to know about them. Beyond these instructions Turner did not go. In three years of working on this project I know of no other significant effort by him to shape editorial content.

Turner's critics have it badly wrong, therefore, when they claim that the series reflects his political views: We were never even told what those might be. All we saw was a remarkable willingness to foot the bill for whatever it would take to make this project a contribution to cold war scholarship as well as to television entertainment. We were therefore able to document the footage we used more thoroughly than has ever been done for a series of this kind. We archived and have made available on-line the complete transcripts of each of the some five hundred interviews featured in it—something else that is unprecedented. And when we de-

2. One critic, who happens to be the editor of this volume, reviewed the series unfavorably solely on the basis of Turner's involvement, without having seen a single episode. See Arnold Beichman, "Cold Water and Cold War Triumphalism," *Washington Times*, January 4, 1998. (See p. 95, this volume, for the full text of the review.)

cided that the originally planned twenty episodes would not be enough—
that we needed more coverage of the cold war in Central America and
Africa, of Sino-Soviet relations, and of espionage—Turner agreed instantly.

Without Turner, there would have been no series in the first place. It
was his idea to begin with. No one else would have had the audacity to
take it on. No one else was waiting in the wings with start-to-finish funding
on a scale sufficient to complete such a project in so short a period of time.
To see the series as a Ted Turner production, therefore, is entirely appro-
priate. To see it as his platform is quite unfair.

So what about the consultants? Did we impose *our* views? We certainly
suggested topics to be covered and people to be interviewed. We reviewed
the scripts of each episode three times: in outline, as rough-cut video, and
in broadcast-ready form. We gave advice freely, and most of the time we
got our way. We were, though, still a committee, which meant that dis-
agreements did occur among us. None of us got everything we wanted,
nor did we have final editorial control. That authority rested, as was clearly
understood from the outset, with Jeremy Isaacs and his production team.[3]
Within these ground rules, we obviously sought to influence the series:
That was our job. Our critics have differed, though, as to just what the
nature of our influence was.

Lloyd Gardner, for example, finds that we emphasized "systemic Soviet weaknesses while faulting the United States mainly for miscalcula-
tions." Bruce Cumings goes further, complaining that *Cold War* presents
its subject "as an open-and-shut case. When you open it, there is Soviet
aggression. And when you close it, there is the aggressor collapsing, courtesy of Margaret Thatcher, Ronald Reagan, and the heroic Mikhail Gorbachev. . . . The good guys defeated the bad guys, even if the cost was
often excessive." This perspective, Cumings maintains, "is closely identified with the one American who played an important role in making the
film, John Lewis Gaddis."

But Jacob Heilbrunn insists that the series "retrospectively accords a

---

3. Despite the fact that some of us, at Sir Jeremy's request, read some draft chapters,
we did not serve as consultants on the book that accompanies the television series. My
comments refer, therefore, only to the documentary.

patina of legitimacy to a Soviet system that was utterly illegitimate" (p. 120 this volume). Charles Krauthammer sees in it "a relentless attempt to find moral equivalence between the two sides" (p. 117 this volume). And then there is Gabriel Schoenfeld, who in an essay negligently titled "Twenty-four Lies about the Cold War"—because he never bothers to say what they were—echoes the objections of Heilbrunn and Krauthammer, concluding: "It beggars the imagination that John Lewis Gaddis, a historian who has shown he knows better, should have lent his name to such an exercise" (p. 30 this volume).

As someone committed to a mushy middle in most historiographical disputations, I will admit to a certain satisfaction in having displeased both Cumings on the left and Schoenfeld on the right. Avoiding extremes is generally better than embracing them. The fact that these two critics came away with such diametrically opposed impressions of the role I am *alleged* to have played, however, reflects an important point about historical "truth": that it exists, to a considerable extent, in the eye of the beholder.

Cumings and Schoenfeld saw the same television series, but they saw it very differently. There is nothing particularly unusual in this: Historians can disagree just as dramatically over the significance of a single document. Such quarrels do not necessarily suggest historical incompetence. They do confirm, though, that historical reality, like its counterparts in paleontology, cartography, and physics, is something we can only approximate—and that even our approximations are subject to revision. This is no trendy, nihilistic postmodernism. It is how hard science and solid history are, and have always been, actually done.

One avoids paralysis in such circumstances by generalizing, and we had to do a lot of that in the documentary. We had to leave much out and simplify what remained, a process that always exasperates specialists, whatever the subject one is gliding over. What we did is no different, though, from what one does when writing a textbook, delivering a lecture, or conducting a seminar. Broad views always blur details.

They are like maps, which highlight the information you need to help you find your way. A road map will differ distinctly from one showing geology, or vegetation, or land use, even if each covers identical terrain. If maps included everything you could possibly encounter along the way—each tree, each rock, each garbage dump—they'd be no help at all.

Historians work similarly in mapping the past, for they must keep in mind the intended audience. The material presented must neither condescend nor confuse; it must inform, but it should not bore. There is always, for any historian, a fine line between the requirements of representation and those of presentation. Television magnifies the problem; it does not change it.

In making *Cold War*, we especially had to remember that we were working in a visual medium. That meant that we could do certain topics better than others: It was easier to represent the Berlin Wall, for example, than it was the Bretton Woods system; we had far more footage on the Hungarian revolution than on the Great Leap Forward. We had to fit what we included within rigid time constraints: Even twenty-four hours is too little to recount in detail a history that extended over twice that many years. And we had to hold the attention of our audience.

We chose to do so by respecting their judgment. We imposed no single interpretive framework but rather allowed multiple voices to be heard. Each episode had its own writer and its own distinctive viewpoint. Each of our interviewees participated in or observed the events recounted; no retrospectively pontificating talking head historians appear anywhere in the series. No doubt we sacrificed clarity by handling things in this way; but we captured more than we otherwise could have of the complexity of events and the ambiguity of human responses to them.

It's clear now that in doing so we made our critics uncomfortable—especially the neoconservatives. Our refusal to tell our audience what to think, together with Turner's injunction to avoid triumphalism, has convinced several of them that we had set out from the start to present the cold war as a "morally equivalent" contest.

As someone who has himself condemned "moral equivalency" in no uncertain terms,[4] I find it odd to be on the receiving end of such a charge. *Cold War* is full of implied and often explicit judgments of both sides. Yet

4. John Lewis Gaddis, "The Tragedy of Cold War History," *Diplomatic History* 17 (winter 1993): 1–16, reprinted in *Foreign Affairs* 73 (January/February 1994): 142–54; "On Moral Equivalency and Cold War History," *Ethics and International Affairs* 10 (1996): 131–48; *We Now Know: Rethinking Cold War History* (New York: Oxford University Press, 1997), pp. 286–87.

no one who sees all its episodes can doubt that the struggle it documents ended in a clear-cut victory for the West, that the illegitimacy of Marxist-Leninist systems brought about that result, and that there are profound moral implications in all of this.

I can only conclude that Heilbrunn, Krauthammer, Schoenfeld, and others like them lack confidence that viewers, if allowed to make up their *own* minds, will reach conclusions similar to theirs. They regard Turner as a left-leaning Pied Piper, seeking to rehabilitate the reputation of old cold war adversaries while beguiling a new generation of students who have no direct experience of that conflict. The only remedy, they seem to be saying, is a rigidly enforced historical orthodoxy.

This is particularly ironic in light of what the neoconservatives were saying—all too accurately—about the Soviet Union during the 1970s and early 1980s. For it was they who then *criticized* a system that insisted on single truths, dogmatically presented—a system that lacked the self-confidence to allow people to view the evidence and make up their own minds. It is almost as if, with the end of the cold war, a kind of panic has set in on the right; there has to be an adversary, and if the Soviet Union is no longer available, then Ted Turner will have to do.

All I can say is, relax, guys. After having now taught this television series to over six hundred Yale undergraduates, I can testify that the last thing they take from it is a belief in moral equivalency. What they do get is an exposure to historical complexity: a sense of how things looked at the time, an awareness of how people who did not know the future attempted to anticipate it, perhaps even the ability to imagine themselves in their place and to ask the tough question: What would I, in similar circumstances, have done? In short, they gain historical maturity.

The role of history should not just be to convey information or impose orthodoxies: It should cultivate critical minds. That requires presenting students with various points of view. It requires leaving them as often disturbed as complacent. It requires asking them to question their values as much as it does congratulating them for holding such values. Indeed it was precisely the absence of that critical perspective that, in the end, proved fatal for Marxist-Leninist regimes in the cold war. It is strange that so many of critics of *Cold War* expected of it a similar ideological rigidity.

3

The Cold War: CNN's Version

Richard Pipes

Richard Pipes is the Baird Research Professor of History at Harvard. His books include *Russia under the Old Regime*, *The Unknown Lenin*, and *The Russian Revolution*.

Sir Jeremy Isaacs, the producer of the ambitious CNN series on the cold war, has proven his ability to turn out first-rate documentary films with a previous series on World War II. The war films were relatively easy to make and relatively noncontroversial in that they depicted an armed conflict pitting young men, most of them draftees, risking their lives, for better or worse causes, but in fair combat. The battlefield is a contest of skill and courage, not an arena of ethics; its objective is clear—to crush the enemy. In this sense, the adversaries are comparable whether in terms of manpower, commanding staffs, weapons, or strategies. Because warfare is physical, not unlike an athletic contest, it lends itself eminently to pictorial presentation.

The cold war, by definition (primarily) a nonmilitary conflict, was something else entirely. It pitted against each other two very different conceptions of life: one that stressed human rights and the rule of law and another that subordinated human rights and law entirely to the interests of the state. In this contest, the rivals, even if they sometimes employed the same means, were not comparable. To render the cold war properly, one must grasp and convey in unequivocal terms the difference between the aims as well as the methods of each side. No one will have any difficulty conceding this point in respect to World War II, when one of the adversaries represented pure evil in word as well as deed. It is somewhat more difficult in the case of the cold war because the Soviet regime, although in deeds not much different from the Nazi one, in rhetoric liked to flaunt Western ideals.

Unfortunately, the producers of the CNN series have chosen to ignore the fundamental disparities between the two camps, treating the conflict as if it were essentially a trial of strength and ruthlessness. The series opens with the familiar picture of the nuclear mushroom and throughout stresses nuclear weapons and the threat of nuclear war as if the struggle were of a military nature, whereas in reality it was a political contest in which both sides wished at all costs to avoid a direct military confrontation. In the press materials distributed with the film prior to its television premiere, the producers summarized the cold war as an "ideological struggle between East and West for world domination." Is this all there was to it? Formulated this way, it should have made little difference which side emerged victorious.

To be sure, the producers of *Cold War* at no point whitewash the communist regimes, at any rate in Europe and Asia. (They are less critical when dealing with their proxies in Africa and Central America). The communist bloc is portrayed as relying on terror and lording it over populations living in poverty and fear. But the reasons for the terror, poverty, and fear are never dealt with. They just happened. The refusal to address this issue mars the entire undertaking, making what was a gigantic conflict over the future of mankind appear as a highly dangerous but ultimately meaningless contest between two bullies.

The failure of the producers to come to grips with the nature of communism and the cold war becomes evident in the first installment. Here, nearly thirty years of Russian history—from the Bolshevik power seizure in 1917 to the end of World War II—are encapsulated in a single hour. This foreshortening of the early history of the Soviet Union is not accidental. It is necessary in order to present the cold war as an "ideological struggle between East and West for world domination," the main responsibility for which, in various subtle ways, is placed on the West.

In fact the cold war began long before nuclear weapons were developed, on October 25–26, 1917, when the Bolshevik Party seized power in the Russian capital and proclaimed its intention of launching civil wars in every corner of the globe to usher in a new era of "proletarian dictatorship." The ultimate objective of the revolution, in the words of Leon Trotsky, Lenin's comrade in arms, was nothing less than "overturning the world." In its official proclamations, the new regime declared war on all existing states by calling on their citizens to emulate the Russians by overthrowing them. This was not mere bluster. The Bolsheviks felt convinced they could not hang on to power in their own country unless they promptly secured the help of Communists in the industrialized as well as colonial countries. Even if they did manage to hold on to power by sheer terror, they feared they would have to ditch their socialist program under the pressure of an antisocialist, "petty-bourgeois" peasantry that happened to constitute 80 percent of Russia's population. In this spirit, Grigorii Zinoviev, the head of the Communist International, boasted in 1919:

> The movement advances with such dizzying speed that one can confi-
> dently say: in a year we shall already forget that Europe had to fight a war
> for Communism because in a year all Europe shall be Communist. And
> the struggle for Communism shall be transferred to America, and perhaps
> also to Asia and other parts of the world.

On coming to power, the Bolsheviks immediately proceeded to subvert neighboring countries. They staged a coup in Finland that the Finns managed to suppress with German military assistance. In Hungary they actually held on to power for half a year until overthrown. In January 1919 they staged a revolution in Germany; it failed, but failure did not stop them from trying again two years later. They also attempted, without success, to establish a communist regime in Persia. In the summer of 1920 they invaded Poland with the view to sovietizing it and using it as a base for the conquest of western Europe. None of these facts is reported on in the CNN series. The omission could not have been due to lack of time, for time is found to depict, in harrowing detail, an eyewitness account of the slow death in the electric chair of Ethel Rosenberg.

After the Poles had crushed the invading Red Army, communist strategy changed. Having concluded that it lacked the power to export its revolution and yet could not count on the support of the foreign "masses," Moscow decided to hunker down within the borders of its reconstituted Soviet empire and promote a world war from which Soviet Russia would abstain in the expectation that the belligerent capitalist powers would exhaust themselves so that Europe would fall into its lap. To this end, Moscow initiated secret military cooperation with Germany, offering the Reichswehr opportunities to circumvent the Treaty of Versailles by testing on Soviet territory the weapons and tactics of the future *Blitzkrieg*. The strategy culminated in the Soviet-Nazi pact of August 1939, which enabled Hitler to start World War II by assuring him that he would not have to fight on two fronts.

None of these early phases of the cold war, without which the events of 1945 and afterward are incomprehensible, is presented in Sir Jeremy Isaac's series. True, the Soviet-Nazi pact of August 1939 is briefly mentioned but casually attributed to Stalin's alleged suspicion of France and Britain following their surrender the previous year at Munich. The fact that, in the 1932 elections, Stalin forbade the German Communists to collaborate with the Social Democrats to stop Hitler goes unmentioned. Because communist ideology and long-term plans are passed over in silence, the viewer has no inkling why in 1945, after having fought loyally side by side for four years, the western Allies and the Soviet Union quarreled and soon turned into bitter enemies. Soviet expansion occurs in a void, as it were. At one point, the narrator explains Stalin's aggressive behavior by fear of "encirclement by the capitalist powers." There is no evidence for this charge: a country of Russia's size is not easily encircled, and indeed no one was attempting to do so.

The unwillingness to confront the fundamental causes of the cold war by contrasting the long-term objectives and methods of the combatants inevitably leads to judgments reflecting "moral equivalence" under which Soviet aggression and Western responses to it are treated as basically identical. This propensity assumes bizarre dimensions in the sixth episode, called "Reds."

Here we are treated to a lengthy account of the Red scare of the 1950s, epitomized by McCarthyism. Senator Joseph McCarthy was, without doubt, a vicious demagogue who exploited widespread fear of communist subversion for his own political ends. But to say this is not to deny that communist subversion existed and was largely ignored by U.S. administrations. Classified documents released in the past few years from both Russian and American archives have revealed the extent to which Soviet agents had penetrated the highest levels of the U.S. government since the 1930s. This evidence is readily available, having been collected and edited by Harvey Klehr and John Earl Haynes in *The Secret World of American Communism* as well as by Allen Weinstein and Alexander Vassiliev in *The*

Haunted Wood: Soviet Espionage in America. Additional evidence to this effect comes from the ultrasecret "Venona Papers," texts of exchanges between Moscow and its U.S. agents intercepted by U.S. intelligence and recently released. Alger Hiss is now known incontrovertibly to have been a Soviet spy rather than the handsome WASP victim of Red hysteria depicted in the CNN film. Paul Robeson, whose harassment is emotionally recounted by his son, was not simply a communist idealist but a Stalinist. The Rosenbergs did betray U.S. atomic secrets to Moscow. The viewer of the CNN series is given no inkling of these facts. He is merely told that many Americans suffered because of a McCarthyite "witch-hunt," which allegedly treated all expressions of dissent as "communism." The "Red Scare" of the 1950s, although it greatly exaggerated the threat of domestic communism, was no witch-hunt.

What makes such misrepresentation doubly objectionable is that it is juxtaposed with the Stalinist postwar terror. To do so is to lose all sense of proportion. No Americans, except two convicted spies, lost their lives as a result of the so-called witch-hunts. In the last years of Stalin, by contrast, millions toiled and perished in the Gulag, while the rest of the population lived in constant dread of arrest. As in the other episodes, the situation in the USSR is candidly presented but, by being coupled with concurrent events in the United States, conveys the totally false impression that there was no significant difference between McCarthyism and Stalinism.

Episode 16—called by the acronym "MAD," for the doctrine of mutual assured destruction formulated in the 1960s by Secretary of Defense Robert McNamara—suffers from the same insidious flaw. It describes accurately the main phases in the evolution of nuclear weapons on both sides, but its recurrent depictions of nuclear mushrooms surging to the sky, bombers taking off, and submarines diving fail to address the fundamental difference in the way the two sides approached nuclear weaponry.

Once the Soviet Union had acquired an arsenal of atomic and hydrogen bombs and the means of delivering them, the U.S. leadership under President Lyndon B. Johnson concluded that these weapons had no utility other than deterrence and abandoned any notion of using them in combat, as dictated by the earlier strategy of "massive retaliation."

This was not the case with the Soviet leadership. In developing nuclear missiles, Moscow proceeded on the assumption that, although they threatened unprecedented destructiveness and for that reason war should be avoided, if, nevertheless, war did break out, they would be an intrinsic component of the military arsenal. Soviet military theorists insisted that technical innovations in weaponry, even of the most revolutionary kind, did not change the nature of warfare: in other words, the more, the better. This was the logic behind Moscow's decision to continue manufacturing and deploying missiles after 1969, when the USSR attained nuclear parity with the United States and when, according to the theory of MAD, it should have frozen its arsenal. We now know from ex-Soviet sources that, in all large-scale military exercises by the Soviet armed forces, resort was had to nuclear weapons. Interestingly, none of the ex-Soviet generals interviewed on CNN accepts the MAD doctrine; all defend missile defenses although, of course, they are incompatible with the concept of mutual assured destruction.

It is hard to know what accounts for the disregard of discussion of Soviet nuclear strategy unless it is the principles of parallelism and equivalence that dog the whole series. Weapons are treated as things in themselves, a mortal threat to life on earth regardless of the mentality of those in charge of them. The concluding message of episode 16 — "Preparations for global annihilation continued" — is out of place, the result of fascination with the military aspects of the cold war, whose whole premise was avoidance of direct military confrontation.

Apparently under the influence of the disarmament movement active in the West during the cold war, the producers of the CNN series tend to reduce the cold war to the arms race and the threat of nuclear Armageddon. This was not the main issue at all. I served for two years in the Reagan White House (1981–82), one of the most stressful periods in U.S.-Soviet relations, as director of East European and Soviet affairs. In this capacity I attended most of the meetings of the National Security Council (NSC) dealing with the communist bloc. I do not recall a single instance when a session of the NSC, at which the president was almost always present, discussed the threat of nuclear war. The meetings were devoted entirely to the political and economic aspects of the conflict with the communist bloc, for they were indeed, to us as well as to our adversaries, their quintessential feature.

The misunderstanding of Soviet motives resurfaces in the account of the invasion of Afghanistan. This campaign, launched to secure for the USSR a bridgehead in the Middle East, close to the Persian Gulf and its oil, is misrepresented as a reaction to NATO's decision to install medium-range missiles known as Pershing 2 in Europe. In reality, the Pershings were a response to an earlier Soviet deployment of SS-20 missiles. The Soviet invasion of Afghanistan had nothing to do with the Pershings. Neither is it correct to claim, as done in the press materials, that "Afghanistan was the U.S.S.R.'s Vietnam." The United States sent half a million men halfway across the world to save a sovereign country from a communist takeover. The Soviet Union sent one hundred thousand men to a neighboring sovereign country to impose on it a communist government. Quite a difference.

The treatment in episode 17 of the two Middle Eastern wars—1967 and 1973—similarly suffers from the failure to discriminate. The Six Day War is depicted as a conflict between Egypt and Israel. The fact that it was an integrated Arab effort, involving, in addition to Egypt, Syria and Jordan, is passed over in silence. So is the fact that it was a war to annihilate the young Jewish state and evict if not slaughter its Jewish population a mere quarter of a century after the Holocaust. The Israeli surprise raid on Egyptian airfields, which in a matter of hours wiped out the Egyptian air force, is labeled a "preemptive strike," although Egypt's closing of the Gulf of Aqaba to Israeli navigation on May 23, 1967, was, by international law, an act of war. The low-intensity but costly in human lives "war of attrition" that followed and in which Soviet pilots directly participated in combat on Egypt's side against Israel goes unmentioned as well. The rest of the reel, dealing with U.S.-Soviet competition in Africa, also fails to discriminate between aggression and response. Its concluding message is, "In the hunt of cold war gains, the superpowers spawned an arms race in the developing world. Their solemn promises of restraint were thrown to the winds."

There is worse to come. Ever sympathetic to Soviet sensitivities to the security of their borders and fears of "encirclement," the CNN series shows no such understanding for U.S. concerns about Soviet penetration south of its border. The reel on the cold war in Central America (episode 18) is one long tale of U.S. bestiality. Left-wing governments and left-wing guerrilla movements in this area are represented as inspired by nothing else than the quest for social justice. They had to struggle against their own right-wing governments and armies loyally backed by Washington and the great corporations with interests in the region (United Fruit, ITT, etc.). They always carried the people with them. And if they did not win, it was because, enjoying only feeble Soviet and Cuban support, they confronted the unflinching enmity of the United States (Fidel Castro adds a comical touch when he says that if the Communists had had a common strategy they would have won the cold war). Thus the narrator intones, "The American dollar and the failures of the armed left crushed Latin American revolutionary dreams."

These are fairy tales. Indisputably, there is a great deal of social injustice in Central America, and the local regimes feel no inhibition in resorting to violence to maintain the status quo. This brutality lends itself to pictorial representation as the political programs, repressive policies, and communist objectives of the left-wing movements do not. The CNN series misses no opportunity to show mutilated corpses of guerrillas and to talk to survivors of the massacres. The deeper reasons for the struggles elude them. The Communists have everywhere and at all times, beginning with the Russian Revolution of 1917, exploited social injustice and national frustrations to come to power and then, on coming to power, promptly restored social injustice and repressed national aspirations. There are brief hints here that the Chileans were miserable under Allende's socialism, but his overthrow and suicide are squarely blamed on native right wingers and foreign "imperialists." No explanation is provided as to why the Nicaraguan Sandanistas lost power in an election, which, in their overconfidence, they had foolishly staged, other than that the U.S. government had allocated $10 million to their opponents. What remains unsaid is that, by virtue of their complete control of the Nicaraguan economy, the Sandanistas disposed of billions of dollars. Nor is any explanation provided as to why, after the fall of the Soviet Union, the alleged "revolutionary dreams" of the people of Latin America evaporated and the guerrilla forces, allegedly fighting for them, laid down their arms.

Astonishing lapses of judgment occur in the treatment of the two administrations of Ronald Reagan (episode 22, "Star Wars," which the producers

chose to focus on his 1983 proposal to install missile defenses, a proposal that was never implemented and hence is little more than a footnote to recent history).

Reagan came into office with a clear program. Although not a learned man, he had the true statesman's intuition. He understood the nature of the conflict with the communist bloc, and he had a sound grasp of the balance of power; instead of allowing himself to be mesmerized by Moscow's military arsenal and paralyzed by the fear of nuclear war, he grasped that the ideological poverty of the USSR and its desperate economic straits made it a weak if blustering opponent. This understanding led him to disregard most of the advice he was receiving. Instead, he formulated an offensive strategy based on the premise that the Soviet system, being incurably sick, could be forced in the direction of reform and possible collapse by a determined military buildup and measures of economic denial, both reinforced by bold rhetoric. He was the first U.S. president to challenge not just Soviet aggression but the communist system itself as its direct cause.

At the time, many in this country and western Europe, not to speak of the Soviet Union, regarded Reagan as a dangerous simpleton capable of unleashing World War III. But his prognoses and the policies based on them proved correct. Although critics warned that his strident anticommunism would harden Soviet behavior and risk a return of Stalinism, the opposite occurred: the Soviet government chose as its leader Mikhail Gorbachev, who adopted a policy of accommodation abroad and reform at home.

None of these historic facts find reflection in the CNN series; indeed, they do not even rate a mention. What we hear and see is the war fright of 1983, when the Soviet leadership, for reasons best known to itself, decided that the United States was about to launch a preemptive nuclear strike on its country (a perfectly inane idea, without any basis in fact, but one that, unintentionally, revealed that the Soviet leadership considered nuclear war entirely feasible). We see hysterical mass antiwar demonstrations in western Europe, without even an allusion to the Soviet money and organization behind them. And at no point is Ronald Reagan given any credit for helping to bring down the Soviet Union and its communist regime. This omission provides a clue to the political framework in which the

CNN series was conceived. (In the words of the *Cold War* book accompanying the series, "Reagan's world was like an old Hollywood movie: he saw things in simple terms of right and wrong, with the Communists as the bad guys and the West leading a crusade for freedom.")

The final installment in the series, called "Conclusions," offers no conclusions. Instead, it shows the last stages of the collapse of communism in Russia and ends with President Bush announcing the cold war over. No insights are given into the nature of the conflict that had kept the world in a state of tension for nearly half a century, and no inferences are drawn from its outcome: Why did the West emerge triumphant? What does its triumph teach us about the limits of efforts to refashion human beings and create an entirely new kind of society—efforts that according to Stephane Courtois, the author of a recently published French book, cost between 85 and 100 million lives. None of these questions is addressed. It is as if the cold war had been nothing more than an athletic contest. And the viewer is left wondering: So what?

To give credit where credit is due, let me say that from a technical point of view the CNN series is masterfully put together. The filmstrips, some of them shown for the first time, are invariably exciting. They are well combined with interviews with many of the leading actors on both sides of the cold war as well as ordinary citizens.

But to a viewer more familiar with the history of the past fifty years the whole enterprise, for all its pretense, seems stillborn. Some of the blame falls on the inherent limitations of the documentary film as a vehicle for conveying complex historical phenomena. It is said that a picture is worth a thousand words, which may be true as far as conveying impressions goes, but understanding requires a different approach. And if deliberately manipulated to impart false impressions, pictures can be positively dangerous. Someone once said that "figures don't lie but liars figure." This can be paraphrased "pictures don't lie but liars picture." The historian, in grappling with the reality of past times, tries to see the whole. In the words of the economic historian Sir John Clapham, he develops "what might be called the statistical sense, the habit of asking in relation to any institution, policy, group, or movement the questions: How large? How long? How often? How representative?" The camera cannot do this. It focuses, of necessity, on the specific, the concrete, the individual, and yet conveys the impression that the singular represents the whole. And because pictures carry great force (unlike words, they do not tax the imagination), they are dangerous means of conveying information.

Even more important, the camera cannot penetrate the human mind and the human heart; it depicts neither motive nor intent but only their physical manifestations, and these look deceptively alike. For this reason, unless great care is exercised, the camera tends to equalize any conflict. A Soviet bomber taking off with a load of nuclear bombs looks strikingly like its American counterpart, much as a Nazi Messerschmidt resembled a Spitfire. But while the Spitfire shielded Britain from a German invasion, the Messerschmidt paved the way for it. Chinese soldiers defending their country from the Japanese do not look much different from Chinese soldiers invading South Korea. The camera cannot convey what really matters, namely, what is in the minds of men, the more so that it is entirely dependent on what the cameramen of the time had access to and what they considered important to record. The inevitable result is emphasis on action with the reasons behind it and its goals at best slurred over or, at worst, ignored.

If this is the case under the best circumstances—when the camera is in the hands of a producer who is both objective and knowledgeable— how much more deceptive can it be when these standards are not met? We end up with a welter of moving pictures that make us feel as if we were in the very midst of historic events, not just as eyewitnesses but almost as vicarious participants, even though we are being manipulated by the se-lection of images.

The CNN series on the cold war is an ominous portent of what we can expect in the future: massive media undertakings carried out with financial means beyond the wildest dreams of scholars and their publishers to impress on the public, with each generation more responsive to visual and aural than to verbal messages, an oversimplified and potentially biased interpretation of historical events. What scholar can hope to supplement his work with such paraphernalia as a web site, manuals and posters for high schools, an accompanying, richly illustrated volume, and a collector's edition of videocassettes distributed by Warner Home Video described as commanding the "largest distribution infrastructure in the global video marketplace"?

The CNN series ultimately panders to the natural propensity of people, especially young people, removed by the passage of time from great historic events, to see these events as meaningless happenings in which the protagonists pretended they were struggling for noble ideals while in fact they were merely pursuing their own selfish aims. This message is insinuated by means of carefully chosen moving pictures and interviews. It is nevertheless false; for just as it did matter that the Athenians defeated the Persians, so it mattered that the West defeated the East in the cold war. And it is a pity that, with the immense resources available to the producers of *Cold War*, they failed to make this obvious but most important point.

4

The Historical Failings of CNN

Robert Conquest

Robert Conquest is a senior research fellow at the Hoover Institution. His books include *The Great Terror, Harvest of Sorrow*, and *Reflections on a Ravaged Century*.

I

When a book is circulated for educational purposes, it needs to meet certain criteria.* Clearly, this is especially so when it is a book on a sensitive and controversial period of modern history. So (a) where more than one interpretation is possible, does the book adequately present all or both? (b) does it ignore, or distort, pertinent data? (c) would it, or any important part of it, impress critical readers as unacceptably superficial? (d) when statements are made on the conduct of two sides in a conflict, is the comparison full and balanced?

When the series on which the book is based appeared on CNN, comments in a number of periodicals from the *Washington Post* to the *New Republic* criticized it for postulating a "moral equivalence" between the West (in particular the United States) and the USSR. The film's sponsors denied this, arguing that the Soviets are shown as behaving far worse than the Americans.

But, critics replied, the two systems were indeed represented as sinning not to the same degree but in much the same way. Whereas, in fact, they were not merely different in degree, as the film (and the book) suggests, they were different in kind. A subsidiary implication is that the book (for we are not here dealing with the film), while not exculpating the Soviet side, clearly and frequently tilts the balance in its favor.

Cold War: An Illustrated History, 1945–1991, companion to the CNN TV series, by Jeremy Isaacs and Taylor Downing (Boston: Little Brown).

II

This can be tested by the book's treatment of individuals. Its view of Lenin, and others of his persuasion, in fact contrasts markedly with its treatment of Western leaders. On Lenin, though it is not denied that the regime he imposed on Russia led to tyranny, he is nevertheless given humanitarian motives: "His socialist principles were meant to ensure decent education, free health care, common ownership of the land, and fairness for all under the tough guidance of the Bolsheviks." Lenin's real attitude to humanity, except in the abstract, is well illustrated by his comment on the 1891–92 famine in Russia, that "psychologically, this talk of feeding the starving masses is nothing but the expression of saccharine-sweet sentimentality characteristic of the intelligentsia." Maxim Gorky was to note that "Lenin has no pity for the mass of the people" and that even "the working class are to Lenin what minerals are to a metallurgist." Many documents are now available in which Lenin insists on mass shootings and hangings. And Bertrand Russell, who met him when he was in power, reports that "his guffaw at the thought of those massacred made my blood run cold."

It might be added that what is wrong is not only the inadequacy of the book's assessment but its simplification of motive beyond the complexities and contradictions inherent in human character. It may, perhaps, also help us to gain a broader view of Lenin if we quote a comment of his on religion (in a letter of November 13, 1913):

> Every religious idea, every idea of God, even flirting with the idea of God, is unutterable vileness . . . of the most dangerous kind, "contagion" of the most abominable kind. Millions of sins, filthy deeds, acts of violence and physical contagions . . . are far less dangerous than the subtle, spiritual idea of God decked out in the smartest "ideological" costumes. . . . Every defence or justification of God, even the most refined, the best intentioned, is a justification of reaction.

Again, when it comes to the Soviet spies Guy Burgess, Donald Maclean, and Kim Philby, we are told that "they acted from political conviction. They believed what they were doing was right." The same could be said of agents of Nazism like John Amery. But, in any case, this is (again) a simplistic point. As Albert Camus long since pointed out, French sympathizers with communism did not love the Soviets so much as they "heartily detested part of the French." On a different point, but again less simplistic, the poet Stephen Spender, who knew the three British spies (and to some extent sympathized with them), noted in his *Journals, 1939–1983*, that

> what they all had was the arrogance of manipulators. . . . Perhaps this was in part because they had voluntarily put themselves at the service of their Russian manipulators . . . their faith in a creed whose mixture of sanctity, bloodiness and snobbery game them a sense of great personal superiority.

When the book deals with Western political figures, we are on different ground. Richard Nixon is shown (in the Hiss case) as motivated solely by ambition. No doubt such ambition played a role, but only an adversarial assessment could fail to consider that he might have had good motives too (but, as we shall see, "anticommunism," unlike "anti-Westernism," would in any case have disqualified him morally).

Ronald Reagan is treated in less hostile, but still hostile fashion, as a simpleton: "Reagan's world was like an old Hollywood movie: he saw things in simple terms of right and wrong, with the Communists as the bad guys." Now regardless of party or political views, this is at the level of caricature and would not be taken as adequate by any serious historian. The opinion of the Soviet ambassador to Washington, Anatoly Dobrynin, is much more positive, and, which is more important, not only more positive but more nuanced. Indeed, Reagan emerges from recent research on his papers (by Kiron Skinner, for instance) as incomparably less shallow than the more or less hostile caricature.

On a further point, whether Reagan is justified, in effect, for seeing the confrontation in "black and white," the CNN writers may disagree with the idea that, when it came down to essentials, the Soviet system was fundamentally hostile to, and concerned to procure the end of, what is usually called the Western democratic culture. But in any case, agree or no, this is, give or take a nuance, the view not merely of simpletons but of major historians in the field. (To be fair, the book's view of Reagan's policies and of his effectiveness changes, indeed contradicts itself, as we proceed.) And, we should note, not only Reagan, but also Harry Truman and George Marshall are treated in the same uninformedly patronizing way.

III

The book begins its chapter on cold war excesses in the United States with a photograph of three people carrying posters demanding the execution of the Rosenbergs. This is evidently intended to be a typical or defining illustration. No serious study of the period, left or right, would assent. The effect, and presumable purpose, is to arouse emotional hostility not merely to those photographed but to all the "anti-Communists" dealt with in the chapter. And, indeed, the book continually speaks of "possessed with hating communism," "witch-hunt," "paranoia," "hysterical." As George Orwell wrote, critics of the Soviet system were called "rabidly anti-Communist." And, he added,

> if from time to time you express a mild distaste for slave-labour camps or one-candidate elections, you are either insane or actuated by the worst motives. In the same way, when Henry Wallace is asked by a newspaper interviewer why he issues falsified versions of his speeches to the press, he replies: "So you are one of those people who are calmouring for war with Russia." There is the milder kind of ridicule that consists in pretending that a reasoned opinion is indistinguishable from an absurd out-of-date prejudice. If you do not like Communism, you are a Red-baiter.

The execution of the Rosenbergs was indeed a major emotional and moral issue. It was, in fact, deplored by many who accepted that the Rosenbergs were guilty of espionage, as of course, in the case of Julius Rosenberg, is no longer denied. But the book's printing of a supposedly psychological explanation, by a hostile defense attorney, of the judge's decision is scarcely a serious contribution.

As to the Rosenbergs' own motives, we are told (p. 42) that they were part of "a network of spies who felt uncomfortable that the United States was the sole owner of the key to atomic warfare." This gives an arguably acceptable motive for their espionage activity, though since they never confessed and thus never advanced such a motive, it is one constructed for them by sympathizers. It has the further disadvantage of being factually untenable. Julius Rosenberg's allegiance to communism dates from before the war, and he entered a Soviet espionage ring in 1942 in connection with technical secrets (radar systems, bombsights, naval gunnery, etc.) and was not until later involved in nuclear matters at all.

The Rosenberg case was indeed highly divisive of American opinion. But its treatment here implies that anticommunist suspicions were all of a knee-jerk nature, a tactic much employed at the time. But this is to distort and destroy legitimate debate. In his *Memoirs*, George Kennan tells us,

> The penetration of American governmental services by members or agents (conscious or otherwise) of the American Communist Party in the late 1930s was not a figment of the imagination of the hysterical right-wingers of a later decade. Stimulated and facilitated by the events of the Depression, particularly on the younger intelligentsia, it really existed, and it assumed proportions which, while never overwhelming, were also not trivial . . . by the end of the war, so far as I can judge from the evidence I have seen, the penetration was quite extensive.

The other matter is that, though it is true that American executive and legislative institutions not only initiated the exposure of some members of the communist espionage rings (many others remain unidentified to this day) but also initiated much publicized persecution of members of the American Communist Party—a campaign we call McCarthyism—Senator Joseph McCarthy disgraced and distorted the real and legitimate public concern. But even in the United States, the attempt to equate anticommunism with McCarthyism is a grave distortion. There were many strong opponents of McCarthyism among the famous American liberal anti-Communists, who waged a strong and powerful struggle against both.

The point is not made here, moreover, that McCarthyism was an American phenomenon only and that countries like Britain, where governments, political parties, and public equally opposed the communist threat, never went through such an experience. On the contrary, the hysteria in Britain—and even more in France—was almost entirely from the anti-anticommunist side!

The details of the Hollywood persecutions are clearly put, but the use of the expression "torture by the Inquisition" may seem excessive, especially if we compare it with, say, a Moscow example from the field of drama. The great producer Vsevolod Meyerhold, then in his sixties, wrote to the prison authorities that he could fortunately put his complaint on paper, as the interrogator Rodos had only broken his left arm (and urinated in his mouth) and, later, on the further beating of his already much-bruised legs, that it felt as if they were being plunged into boiling water. After months of this, he was shot.

By the best Western standards, the Hollywood enquiry was nevertheless an excess. One of the factors in this and other cases that the book does not present is, however, the nature of the Communist Party USA (CPUSA). Not a political party in the ordinary sense, it was (with several million dollars and until the late 1980s) heavily financed by Moscow (as is now fully documented). Whatever else its members sought, they were required to give full and uncritical support to all Soviet actions.

During the earlier part of World War II, before the Nazi invasion of Russia, the CPUSA exerted its power in certain trade unions to prevent aid to Britain. From 1941 it urged the persecution of anti-Soviet left-wing groups, such as the Trotskyites, appealing to the U.S. authorities to arrest and suppress these other radicals. The CPUSA joined in the denunciations of the Yugoslav Communists when, in 1948, these threw off Moscow's control. And so on.

The other point about the Communist Party that is relevant is that it was run on Leninist principles, with all decisions of the center automatically binding on members and with the equally Leninist corollary that all methods of infiltrating and defeating enemies were legitimate. Many ordinary members of the party were people of goodwill with radical views, and most could not in the long run stomach its tactics. But active members often found themselves, as it were, trapped in takeover power plays in the larger groups to which they belonged, in Hollywood as elsewhere.

Thus, though the House Un-American Activities Committee and other committees victimized Communists, and are understandably reprobated, there is (as is now generally recognized) another aspect to all this. At any rate, here again we find not the "black-and-white" picture presented by the book but, in many cases, a real moral dilemma. Those disillusioned members of the CP who thought that true accounts should be given and "named names" are simply presented as the equivalent of school snitches. But they too thought they were carrying out a moral duty and were themselves the subject of various persecutions over the years—though we can now record that this is largely forgotten and forgiven even in Hollywood. And as to the substance of the matter, Arthur Schlesinger Jr. has lately pointed out that such criteria would not have been applied to similar "betrayals" by former members of American Nazi movements.

Much the same could be said of how, as the great physicist and democrat Andrei Sakharov put it, the American scientific community treated Edward Teller "meanly" and of the treatment of others in the intellectual world who had done what they felt to be their duty. Here again the old feuds seem to be dying out among the intellectual public—though still pursued by such productions as this book. Some of these points may indeed be arguable. But they are not treated as even arguable in the book, which takes a simple and partisan view.

Then again, the Kent State killings were a tragedy and a blot on the record of the United States. To say this is to judge it, quite rightly, by American standards. But such events in other countries are judged by different standards, and this is precisely what makes nonsense of the theme that both the democratic and communist countries sinned or erred. Four students were killed at Kent State by panicky National Guards, at once ordered by their officers to stop. The book quotes a commission report that "a nation driven to use the weapons of war upon its youth is a nation on the edge of chaos." This is, of course, misleading hyperbole—it was not a "nation" that was responsible, nor did it attack its "youth"—phrases that might be more applicable to Tiananmen Square. That the sponsor of the book, and the film, Ted Turner, lately said that Kent State and Tiananmen Square are wholly comparable is enough of a comment on this point. But again, such attitudes are not compatible with any normal educational criteria of knowledge and judgment.

IV

In the reasons the book gave for the confrontation we call the cold war, the main omission is a vital one. That is, the conception that the Marxist-Leninist creed saw the world as a scene of essential antagonisms and insisted that the conflict must be pursued until the overthrow of the noncommunist order the world over. This motivation has been confirmed in the memories of four Politburo members, by post-Soviet foreign ministers and others and was only abandoned by the last Soviet foreign minister, Edvard Shevardnadze, in 1990.

Cold War's presentation of what is after all its central theme is notably different from that advanced in its leading U.S. historical adviser's book on the subject, *We Now Know*, by John Lewis Gaddis, in which he describes the attempts by prominent Soviet officials to persuade Stalin to initiate at least a period of comparative cooperation with the West. Gaddis quotes Maxim Litvinov, then Soviet deputy foreign minister, who was asked by the American envoy Averell Harriman, in November 1945, what the West could do to satisfy Stalin and answered, "Nothing." In June 1946, still in that post, he warned a Western journalist that the "root cause" of the confrontation then reached was "the ideological conception prevailing here that conflict between the Communist and capitalist worlds is inevitable"—that is, no more than the doctrine long since announced by Lenin that "a series of frightful clashes" were bound to occur between the two systems, leading finally to world victory of communism. When the correspondent asked Litvinov, "Suppose the West would suddenly give in and grant all Moscow's demands? . . . would that lead to goodwill and the easing of the present tension?" Litvinov answered, "It would lead to the West being faced, after a more or less short time, with the next series of demands." The book simply implies, and that in a shallow and superficial fashion, that all Stalin wanted was a buffer area between him and the West.

v

On the broader scale, the conflict is represented here as one between two "ideologies"—sometimes defined as capitalist versus communist; that is, in a sort of balance.

But this is to misuse the word ideology and thus to avoid the difference between the pluralist and totalitarian viewpoints. Totalitarianism, to be sure, is a word largely avoided by the book when it deals with Stalinism, though it was used of the Soviet order by both Gorbachev and Yeltsin and found adequate by such famed scholars as Leszek Kolakowski and Gio-

vanni Sartori and by many others of major repute like the French historian
François Furet.

Ideology is not a clearly defined word. But its normal meaning at least
is as a single, unified worldview. Marxism-Leninism is such a phenomenon. But capitalism is a description of an economic system.

The political and intellectual figures in the West did not have a closed
or unified "ideology." They included conservatives and socialists, Chris-
tians and atheists, liberals and nationalists, in almost all cases people with
only general views on present and future policies and a willingness to
compromise with and work with the others who did not share their phi-
losophies. The West, that is, was not in any normal sense "ideological,"
and the use of the word to cover two such essentially different things is a
major distortion.

It is worth noting in this context that socialists and social democrats
were among the strongest opponents of Soviet power, and of their own
countries' communist movements.

VI

The foreign policies of the West are also subjected to what can only be
called misrepresentation from very early on, when allied "intervention" in
Russia in 1918–1919 is presented as a major effort to overthrow the Soviet
regime and one that had a permanent impact on Moscow's attitudes.

Now, first of all the American "intervention" was minimal, and U.S.
troops had only one minor skirmish with local Bolsheviks. The British
intervention, a couple of brigades, was larger. Asked in by the Soviets to
block German presence in the far north, they were briefly in action against
the Bolsheviks, but then total casualties were a few hundred, some of them
against non-Bolshevik forces. It is true that history as taught under Stalin
made much of the "intervention," though the American component was
scarcely mentioned until it became politically suitable, in the 1940s. And
no serious scholar accepts the view put forward in this book.

It is true, of course, that the Allies supported the anti-Bolshevik regimes
in the civil war, including those based on the majority of the elected
Constituent Assembly that Lenin had forcibly dissolved. It is equally relevant that Lenin regarded the whole struggle as part of an international
revolution to be exported as and where possible, with attempts to capture

Warsaw, the crushing of the social-democratic Georgian republic, and so on.

When it comes to the cold war period we continually find such expressions as, after the communist seizure of power in Prague, "Washington deliberately fanned the flames of anti-Communism," or, to put it another way, rallied opposition to the action.

Again, intemperate remarks by Western politicians and others are prominently figured. The far more pervasive and continual Soviet denunciations of bloodthirsty Western imperialism, with endless cartoons of Uncle Sam and John Bull wallowing in blood, and with teeth like bayonets right into the 1980s, hardly figure. And as to revealing remarks, it is odd not to find Stalin's telling the Yugoslav leaders in April 1945, "The war will soon be over. We shall recover in fifteen to twenty years, and then we'll have another go at it."

Much space is devoted to the reliance by the United States, in some areas, on authoritarian allies. I recall similar circumstances in World War II, when Britain was long alone but for the Metaxas dictatorship in Greece (which won the first victory over fascism), some French colonial regimes, and the feudal Ethiopian emperor (reimposed by British troops). And later the United Kingdom, and the United States, had to rely on an ally even worse from a democratic point of view—Stalin. In an ideal world we could perhaps insist on a better line. But while some reactionary regimes were useful, the Western Alliance included all the major democracies.

More than once, the book uses expressions like "left-leaning governments" as the targets of American policy. This is an evasion. Many left-leaning governments, such as the socialist ones in Britain, Norway, Germany, and elsewhere, were among America's stoutest allies. "Left-leaning" in the book's terms is therefore a code word for "pro-Soviet"—quite a different thing.

Much space is devoted to American support for the anticommunist parties and trade unions, left and right, in Italy, France, and elsewhere with, again, the Communists represented in a favorable light. We are told that Italian communist leader Palmiro Togliatti had "spent the war years in Moscow, he was no stooge of the Kremlin," and sought to develop a form of communism suited to Italy and opposed to tyranny, a program that appealed to many. This is followed by an account of the American financial and other assistance to the noncommunist democratic parties in Italy's 1947 elections.

As to facts, Togliatti had been in Moscow not merely in the war, but as one of the half dozen top leaders of the Stalinist Communist International, from the early 1930s, sponsoring many of its lethal purges. After Stalin's death in 1953, he developed a rather independent stance, but until then he remained totally committed to the Soviet Union.

The program he put forward in 1947 did indeed appeal to a large public. So did the program of the Czechoslovak Communist Party before it took power, when it imposed one of the worst of the Stalinist dictatorships. The implication that Togliatti could simply be trusted is a strange one.

The Americans are nevertheless presented as putting unfair pressure on, or exerting unfair influence on, the Italian electorate—mainly by financial means. It is not mentioned that the Italian Communist Party was itself heavily financed by the Soviets.

A further point is that after the election the Italian Communist Party remained free to operate, while in every country where a communist regime had come to power, whether through elections or otherwise, the democratic parties had all been suppressed and their leaders killed or jailed. They too had promised liberty—indeed liberty for all antifascist parties was guaranteed in the Hungarian, Romanian, and Bulgarian peace treaties.

A number of the book's stances are not merely misleading but are no longer accepted in serious circles even by those who agree with its general political views. For example, the contras in Nicaragua, depicted here as little more than CIA-sponsored reactionary terror groups, are now recognized by former supporters of this thesis as a genuine resistance movement, with many ex-Sandinistas in their ranks. And then much is made of American financing of anti-Sandinistas in the Nicaraguan election of 1990. But the local media and virtually all instruments of persuasion and power remained in Sandinista hands—opposition posters were only to be seen by the road from the airport into town, as a sight for foreign visitors.

The book's treatment of Chile is another example. The United States had long since (under Presidents Kennedy and Johnson) funded various moderate papers and organizations. Nixon, as the book rightly notes (and as most people rightly condemn) gave instructions to a reluctant CIA to find and support generals for a military coup to preempt Allende's election, a project fairly soon abandoned. Although the book's passage on this is muddled and confused, it gives the impression that the United States, or the CIA, was involved in the later, and successful, coup by General Pinochet; but this, as has long been known, was kept entirely secret from the American government. Then much is made of the supposedly U.S.-sponsored overthrow of a "democratically elected government." But one does not have to be a partisan of the Pinochet regime to point out that this is historically misleading—quite apart from the fact that to be democratically elected is in itself a criterion that was similarly satisfied by Hitler.

Allende got more than a third of the votes but was only "elected" when the moderate party agreed to add theirs to his on the condition of his observing the constitution. It was not long before both the Chilean Supreme Court and Parliament were ruling that he was in breach of that constitution. And when the coup took place, the majority parties welcomed it—though soon withdrawing their support for General Pinochet as he instituted military rule.

In the international context, the book's major villian is the CIA.

No one, one takes it, would deny that the CIA produced both errors and morally dubious actions. There are, however, two points largely absent from the book. First, the CIA was under direct orders from successive presidents and obliged to carry them out. Then, it was the only channel through which American secret funds could be deployed abroad.

On its failings within its assignment, of course, such objections can be made to all organizations in the real world. On the moral issue—and not only in this context—historians are divided. Just as in actual warfare—and particularly in one with aerial bombardment—innocents are killed, and things can go wrong, but all except true pacifists nevertheless in some cases support military action as sometimes the least bad option. The same criteria, many historians would argue, applies to covert action. At any rate, the book presents an indictment rather than noting such defense of a series of American presidents and their agencies.

VII

A constant theme is that Moscow had a legitimate fear of Western aggression. We are told, for example, that a million U.S. troops abroad were "all threatening the Soviet Union."

They were of course much outnumbered by the Soviet army; more telling yet is the fact that right up to the end, the communist armies in East Germany were on short notice to invade the West, while NATO troop deployment was wholly defensive.

VIII

For a book this size, and with this theme, there is notable inadequacy on the issue of nuclear weapons. For example, it might have been thought evidential to include the fact that, in 1948, although the United Nations Scientific and Technical Committee, to which the question of atomic development was referred and which included Russian and Polish scientists and the French communist professor Joliot-Curie, reported unanimously in September 1946 that inspection and control over the whole process of production was desirable and technically possible, the Soviet representatives rejected all plans incorporating this view as "an assault on State sovereignty" (Vyshinsky in the General Assembly, November 9, 1948) and insisted on such limitations as were incompatible with the report of the Scientific Committee. As Vyshinsky in the Political Committee on November 10, 1949, put it: "We are not obliged to subordinate ourselves or to render an account in this manner to any international organs."

More strikingly, on the development of the hydrogen bomb, we are told that Truman's decision to go ahead with it "fired the starter's pistol for the ultimate arms race." But as the USSR's leading nuclear physicist, Andrei Sakharov, points out, the USSR was going ahead with the bomb development regardless of American work on it—and the book itself notes that in fact Moscow achieved a deliverable bomb before the United States did.

A further relevant point is the whole chapter on MAD—the concept of mutual assured destruction. This doctrine—that the threat of instant retaliation would deter either the USSR or the United States from a first strike—is, of course, defensible, even though (equally of course) criticizable. But it is accompanied by the argument that to seek methods of defense is destabilizing. This involves what can only be called a one-sided consideration of Reagan's Strategic Defense Initiative (SDI) (erroneously described here as promising total interception). But in fact it was the prospect of SDI, though also of the general American technological lead, (as the book contradictorily admits), that made what Gorbachev called the "insane militarization" of the USSR no longer tenable.

IX

For a book that goes into great detail on some matters, we also find a great deal of mere sloppiness, especially on Soviet phenomena. To take the details of a single page: I find a box with the title "Beria: Stalin's Evil Genius," the implication being that he led Stalin into wicked ways. The justification for this is that the document we have on the execution of some 25,000 Poles in March–April 1940 is a formal application by Beria, as head of the NKVD, to Stalin for permission to shoot them. No serious historian has any doubt that the initiative was Stalin's. Beria was indeed, like all Stalin's police chiefs, an instrument of terror. But at least after Stalin's death he reversed the anti-Semitic purge. His colleagues later had him arrested and shot, but there is no evidence at all that (as stated here) he had planned to seize power. And the circumstance of his trial and execution are not (as the book says) obscure, but fully documented. On the same page, we find it stated that the victims of the "Doctors Plot" were arrested in January 1953: they had been arrested the previous year, the case was *announced* in January 1953. And it puts into the same sentence the arrest of Stalin's sisters-in-law that had taken place several years earlier. Moreover, while the best part of a paragraph is here given to Stalin's appearance at the Nineteenth Party Congress in October 1952, only one sentence covers the crucial trial of the Jewish Anti-Fascist Committee a few months earlier, and merely says that ten leading Jews (in fact thirteen) were shot for "Jewish nationalism." They were shot on a wide variety of charges; they were tortured over several months; they included the leading Jewish literary figures—and the book omits the fate of the USSR's most prominent Jew of all, Solomon Mikhoels, who was simply murdered on Stalin's orders by prominent secret police officials. All these errors appear on a single page. Many more pages could be similarly criticized.

x

In a long book supposedly exploring every aspect of the cold war we may conclude by noting it is strange to find one phenomenon of some significance in covering American attitudes to the cold war and to the Soviet Union not treated here. That is, the position of the American media. One has only to note that a recent Nexus search of American newspapers in the postwar period reveals the word "bellicose" applied to Reagan 211 times, to Margaret Thatcher 41 times, and to Brezhnev 5 times—this in a period covering the launching of the Afghan war. This attitude seems to have some application to this book and, of course, to its media sponsor.

5

Mules, Missiles, and McCarthy: CNN's *Cold War*

Thomas M. Nichols

Thomas M. Nichols is an associate professor of strategy, Naval War College, and an associate of the Davis Center for Russian Studies, Harvard University. This article first appeared in *International Journal* 54, no. 3 (summer 1999).

The casual viewer of CNN's twenty-four-part *Cold War* series will come away convinced of at least three things: nuclear missiles are horribly dangerous, Joseph McCarthy was nearly as bad as Joseph Stalin, and American mules are much bigger and stronger than Greek mules. This last bit of information is worth noting because *Cold War* seems to think it was important: In an episode ostensibly devoted to the Marshall Plan and the origins of the cold war in the late 1940s, the producers spent more than a few baffling minutes of airtime on Greek peasants who attested firmly that the mules sent from the United States to replace those lost in the war were more than adequate. "The mules were very good," a Greek farmer tells the off-camera interviewer. "They were fat and big. And we began to use the mules to plow."

The attention devoted to mules is, of course, part of *Cold War*'s attempt to tell the epic tale of the confrontation between East and West through the stories of people, both exalted and ordinary. It fails, not least because this disruptive shift in emphasis from presidents and premiers to students and workers comes at the expense of more substantive issues, which are, in the end, left unexplored. It is not particularly interesting (even if it is a surprise to younger viewers) to note that many citizens of both the East and the West lived in fear during the cold war—and, as if to make the point repeatedly, the series is replete with ominous music and exploding

The views expressed are solely those of the author and not of the government of the United States.

mushroom clouds—nor does it add to our understanding of the cold war merely to emphasize that it scared a great many people.

Nonetheless, the series is worth watching if only for the startling visual detail in which it renders an era, especially with spectacular color footage from the Soviet bloc unseen until now. The interviews with top officials from both East and West are likewise fascinating, and *Cold War* will probably stand as the last film record of the reminiscences of people like Clark Clifford, Anatoly Dobrynin, and even Fidel Castro. An academic audience will find interesting details and useful comments scattered here and there throughout these interviews and film clips. (Episodes on spies, China, and *Sputnik* stand out here.)

But for those viewers who are not specialists in history or politics, *Cold War* obscures more than it explains. The series is organized thematically rather than chronologically (although there is a loose march from 1945 to 1991 across the episodes), which not only undermines any sense of continuity to the history of the conflict but also removes important events from their context. Moreover, most episodes are written in oddly stilted, indirect language that makes those same events seem merely to happen rather than to have been caused by either superpower.

The use of a disorderly structure and overly judicious tone is not accidental. It is meant to present *Cold War*'s thesis of moral equivalence between East and West with understatement and by implication. The producers would no doubt argue that they strove for balance, and they have achieved it: The Soviet Union and the United States seem equally culpable in prosecuting the cold war (although the clear credit for its end is given to Mikhail Gorbachev). If there is an underlying "plot" to *Cold War*, it is this: The Soviet Union was an insecure state that mostly wanted to be left alone and whose intentions were misunderstood, whereas the United States—blessed with material prosperity the likes of which those in the Soviet Union could only dream about—consistently failed to grasp the innate weakness and deeply fearful nature of its enemy. (Oh, and yes, thank heaven for Gorbachev.) If this were presented clearly as the editorial viewpoint, it might have served to strengthen the series as a teaching tool or a source of debate. Instead, *Cold War* tries to establish its position by sleight of hand, using careful wording and misleading editing rather than simply admitting its bias from the outset.

Other critics of this series have pointed out in detail the moral parallel the series draws between the United States and the Soviet Union, but few have noted the Orwellian style employed to reorder events and obscure responsibility for crucial moments in the cold war. This misdirection makes it especially problematic for classroom use since conscientious teachers will find that if they use the series in class they will have to draw up a lecture just to fill the blank spots or to correct the misleading characterizations in each episode. Some specific examples are particularly telling.

"The Soviet Union," the program tells us early on, "offered an alternative model for society: public ownership and a centrally planned economy, in contrast to the Western belief in a mixed economy and free trade." But this episode, entitled "Marshall Plan," is set in the late 1940s and not, as one might expect from talk of "alternative models," in the 1960s. The idea that Stalinist Russia was offering an "alternative" is difficult enough to accept, but it is even harder to imagine that this was so seductive to Europeans that it forced President Harry Truman (in the words of *Cold War*'s writers) to "pitch" the Marshall Plan "as a struggle between freedom and tyranny"—as though that was not what it was.

The program duly notes that poverty was indeed a potential breeding ground for communism and that the Marshall Plan was meant to feed and reconstruct Europe, but it also dutifully includes commentary by French scholar Marianne Debouzy that "most people" felt American aid was "self-serving." For those who might have missed the point, the episode ends by noting that America's attempts to build a "European consumer society" meant the Soviet Union was "forced to build its own rival bloc. The people of the socialist countries would eye the West for 40 years . . . and wonder." And wonder what, exactly? Why poor Joseph Stalin was scared by Western capitalists into being "forced" to make a prison camp of Eastern Europe? It is difficult to imagine a casual viewer coming away from this episode with an understanding of the origins of the cold war in anything but economic, even imperialist, terms. But as later episodes indicate, this was not the last terrible act Stalin or his successors would be "forced" to commit.

The episode entitled "Reds" begins with a declaration that in the 1950s "both sides turned their fear inwards against their own people. They hunted the enemy within." The narrative and imagery then juxtapose the story of the ruined careers of Hollywood screenwriters with the millions of lives extinguished in the Soviet camps. The moral equivocation is stunning, but just as important is the way it is accomplished: Combining events in the USSR and the United States in the same episode allows the series to pay relatively less attention to the Gulag—Stalin's crimes are admitted but not dwelt on and then are mitigated because they are presented in tandem with footage of the glowering senator from Wisconsin. The audience is presumably left to draw its own conclusions, but it is hard to imagine that they will not reach the one *Cold War* strives so nimbly to present.

Later episodes are little better. The 1960s in America are presented in an episode called "Make Love Not War," a truly bizarre interlude in the series that is less a discussion of the cold war than an excursion into the American counterculture of the 1960s. There is plenty of material about campus protests (as though these had some larger effect on the cold war) and the struggle for civil rights, as well as wisdom from such unlikely figures of the cold war as Allen Ginsberg, Hugh Hefner, and Dick Gregory. The entire episode is shot through with cynical disdain for the United States and reverence for the various defunct movements of the 1960s (in a sad and ironic moment, the late Abbie Hoffman is seen proclaiming a "second American Revolution" that is "winning"). Although this view of the decade is prevalent among nostalgic leftists, it is unclear what, if anything, it has to do with the cold war.

As the series moves ahead to the 1970s and 1980s, the thin pretense of balance begins to unravel. The episode on Vietnam says little about internal Soviet or Chinese deliberations but takes care to finish by noting Richard Nixon's advice to the South Vietnamese at the Paris talks to hang tough and wait for a better deal under a Republican administration. As journalists often point out, the bias of a story is most often revealed in its final sentence, and this episode ends (on the heels of the Nixon story and footage first of Nixon and then of a military funeral) with the somber comment that "America's war in Vietnam was to last another four years." Of course, there was no breakthrough imminent in Paris, but the moral is clear: Nixon, not Lyndon Johnson, and certainly not Ho Chi Minh, Leonid Brezhnev, or Mao Tse-tung, is the real villain behind the tragedy in Vietnam. (To be fair, "Make Love Not War" insists on referring to Vietnam as

"Johnson's war," but it is Nixon, not Johnson, who lurks in the background of several *Cold War* episodes.)

The episode on détente is not actually about détente but is rather a second episode about Vietnam. The obvious intention is to link the policy of détente to the disaster Nixon inherited from LBJ, and although it is true that Nixon saw better relations with the Soviet Union as something that would help extricate the United States from Vietnam, there was much more to this policy and what it meant in Washington and Moscow. But this is left aside in the eagerness to show the Kent State shootings, to dwell on the bureaucratic infighting in Washington (the Kremlin had no such struggles, apparently) and the Watergate scandal. There is nothing about the origins of détente, other than a glossy and brief nod to Germany's Willy Brandt, and almost nothing about the impact it had—or, more precisely, failed to have—on the arms race. There is no mention of the fact that the establishment of détente was followed by a severe crisis precipitated by the Soviet intention to intervene in the 1973 Arab-Israeli war, or the deployment in 1975 of the Soviet SS-18 missile (which itself was a dramatic turn in the arms race that détente was supposed to have dampened). In fact, there is almost nothing at all about the superpower relationship but quite a bit about the turmoil in America.

What discussion there is of the cold war in this period is troubling. The Soviet Union, we are told, was avidly in favor of détente because "where memorials kept alive the remembrance of a terrible war, détente had few enemies." But détente, as we knew even in the 1970s, had plenty of enemies even in the Soviet regime. Viewers, however, do not get a sense of the full scope of aggressive Soviet policies in the 1970s and early 1980s because the entire period is split among several episodes; as a result, the USSR is never seen as the West saw it by 1980—spread across the Third World, bristling with newly deployed long-range and theater nuclear weapons at home, and at war in Afghanistan. The full impact of Soviet policies in the 1970s is thus lost, and by the time Ronald Reagan is elected after excoriating Jimmy Carter's stumbling foreign policy, the audience might well wonder what all the fuss in Washington was about.

Other important issues of the latter period of the cold war are left aside, supposedly in the name of telling the stories of the lives of ordinary citizens. Thus the SS-20 issue, perhaps one of the pivotal moments in the

cold war, is abbreviated in favor of comments from obscure Carter campaign workers and footage of gasoline lines. (The gas lines are shown
because the episode, "Freeze," tries to leave the impression that the crisis
in Iran was responsible for the state of the United States economy in 1979
and thus of some relevance to the cold war, an interpretive stretch to say
the least.)

The series finally collapses and surrenders to its own bias in discussing
the 1980s. The episode on the Reagan years is titled, tellingly, "Star Wars,"
as if this were the only policy of consequence between 1981 and 1988. It
opens to the strains of "Stand By Your Man" and the cornpone drawl of a
"Reagan supporter" named Doc and indulges the caricature of Ronald
Reagan as a rather dim if affable man. Gorbachev, by contrast, comes
across as a suave intellectual who recalls his first impression of Reagan as
a "caveman." (Would that he had spent as much time thinking about the
personal qualities of Marshal Dmitrii Yazov or the other retrograde coup
plotters with whom he surrounded himself.)

A great deal happened between the superpowers during the 1980s, of
course, but not so much that the episode couldn't spare valuable airtime
(at the expense of more important issues) for a shameless plug about the
1986 Goodwill Games—a reminder that the series is, after all, airing on
Ted Turner's network. Insofar as it does cover more substantial moments
of the decade, the narrative is quite misleading, and it is here that *Cold
War*'s tendency to misdirect its audience is most evident.

Viewers are told about the following events in the following order:
Reagan's "evil empire" speech, the speech announcing the Strategic Defense Initiative (SDI), Yuri Andropov's accession to the Soviet leadership,
a worldwide KGB nuclear war alert, increased United States' spy flights
with aircraft that "looked like civilian airliners and often flew close to
passenger routes," the shooting down of Korean Airlines flight 007, arms
control talks in Geneva being "broken off" (as though this just happened,
like a freak storm or car accident), and the "zero option" for removing
nuclear weapons from Europe and its rejection by Brezhnev and eventual
acceptance by Gorbachev. The story line is clear: Reagan came to office
and scared the daylights out of the Soviet leaders, who promptly went on
alert (nearly starting World War III) and were so paranoid they accidentally

shot down an airliner. Arms talks then somehow collapsed but were later saved by Gorbachev.

The actual chain of events is quite different. The worldwide war alert began under Brezhnev in 1981, the same year that Reagan's zero option was proposed and rejected. Andropov came to power a year later. A year after that, Reagan made his "evil empire" and SDI speeches. Six months later, KAL 007 was shot down (and not by accident). Andropov was, by some accounts, shocked at the international outpouring of antipathy to the USSR and gave up any hope of relaxing East-West tensions. Arms talks in Geneva were not "broken off"; the Soviet delegation walked out of them. In other words, a proper portrayal of these crucial years (especially if it had followed a coherent presentation of the 1970s) would have suggested the exact opposite interpretation of that taken in *Cold War*: The Soviet regime was not a victim of Reaganism; rather, Reaganism was a response to Soviet mischief and aggressiveness.

The episode ends by noting that, by 1988, Reagan and Gorbachev had "together . . . seized their chance" for peace. But this glosses over the fact that the Soviet Union had little alternative but to go along with the chance seized by the Americans. The comity the superpowers found in arms control did not extend to other arenas (this is left unsaid in this episode but mentioned in others), and by 1987 the USSR was being hard-pressed around the world by the Americans, especially in Afghanistan. Although the episode shows footage of the squalling Greenham Common women being dragged away from NATO bases by police, the fact is that by the late 1980s Reagan and Margaret Thatcher, not the protesters or the Kremlin, had won the propaganda fight in Europe. (Even some Soviet writers later admitted that they felt they had overestimated the potential of the peace movement, a point left out of *Cold War*.) America was awash in wealth and backed by a renewed unity in NATO; the Soviet Union was flat broke, falling behind technologically, and barely able to hold the Warsaw pact together. In sum, to say that Reagan and Gorbachev seized an opportunity together implies that the United States and the USSR were on an equal footing, and this was obviously not the case. Equally obvious was the reluctance of *Cold War*'s producers to say so.

This careful protection of Gorbachev is carried over to the episodes on the fall of communism and the dissolution of the USSR, both of which neatly sidestep Gorbachev's incompetence at home and abroad. When Soviet bloc states went into revolt, Gorbachev is presented as stoically accepting this as the price of reform—rather than as a hapless bystander to events he had put in motion and did not now comprehend. Likewise, Soviet tanks in Lithuania are not *ordered* to kill Soviet citizens, but instead they "attacked," as if with minds of their own. Nowhere is Gorbachev's culpability even hinted at. (Indeed, he is described as "caught in the middle," but the middle of what is left unspoken.)

The last episode closes with a few bright spots. Although the series insists again that "Gorbachev had done as much as anyone to end the cold war," the last words go to Vaclav Havel and George Bush. But even these nods to the noble dissident and the prudent president are not enough to redeem the previous twenty-four hours of equivocation and obfuscation.

In the end, *Cold War* is an achievement in filmmaking but little more. Crisply photographed—the episode on spies, for example, shot all its interview subjects in semidarkness, a subtle but effective touch—and beautifully narrated by actor Kenneth Branagh, it is a first-rate production. (The opening credits might be one of the best title sequences ever made for television: against the show's stirring theme music, a group of people with flashlights peer down a dank hallway as images of the cold war flash by on the walls, an evocative sequence that symbolizes perfectly the search for the hidden past.) As history, however, it is incomplete because in the end it is a political, rather than a historical, project. It is unsuitable for either the classroom or the living room; given the obvious expense and care that went into it, this is a pity. But the myth of moral equivalence that currently surrounds the cold war is a tenacious one, and hardly needs twenty-four weeks of glossy television to bolster it.

6

Why We Were in Central America

Mark Falcoff

Mark Falcoff is a resident scholar at the American Enterprise Institute in Washington, D.C. The author of numerous books and articles on Latin America, he served on the staffs of both the Senate Foreign Relations Committee and the Kissinger Commission on Central America during the Reagan administration. This article first appeared in *Commentary*, May 1999. Reprinted with permission. All rights reserved.

Speaking in the capital of Guatemala on March 10, 1999, President Bill Clinton formally apologized for the role the United States had played in that country and, by extension, for our past policies throughout Central America. His exact words were these:

> For the United States, it is important that I state clearly that support for military forces and intelligence units which engaged in violence and widespread repression was wrong, and that the United States must not repeat that mistake.

The president's dramatic apology, offered during a tour of four Central American republics, was not the only event this past March that, almost a decade after the guns fell silent in Central America's civil/international wars, reopened the issue of American involvement in that part of the world. Another was the publication of the report of the Historical Clarification Commission in Guatemala, which investigated repression of native communities (and others) during the country's long internal war. And still another was the release by the Washington-based National Security Archive of recently declassified documents that also related to U.S. involvement in Guatemala. Finally, there was "Our Own Backyard," an episode of the CNN series *Cold War*, that portrayed the U.S. role in the region in an extremely harsh light.

The report of the Clarification Commission alone, covering a period from roughly 1954, when a CIA-sponsored coup ousted the government of Jacobo Arbenz, to 1991, when the Guatemalan government signed a

peace accord with the guerrilla forces seeking to overthrow it, was enough
to curl one's hair and was duly hailed in the American and European press
as proof positive of Washington's long-term perfidy. The commission,
according to the (London) *Guardian,* concluded that "the U.S. was responsible for most of the human-rights abuses committed during the 36-
year war in which 200,000 people died." And the *Guardian* report continued, in a graphic vein:

> A 1966 document reveals that U. S. security forces set up a safe house
> inside the presidential palace in Guatemala City for use by Guatemalan
> security agents and their U.S. contacts. It became the headquarters for
> the so-called "dirty war." Another document reveals security forces ar-
> rested 32 people suspected of aiding the guerrillas. A CIA cable a year
> later identified some of the missing as people on a list of "Guatemalan
> Communists and terrorists" who were "executed secretly by Guatemalan
> authorities." In October 1967, a secret State Department cable said covert
> Guatemalan security operations included "kidnapping, torture, and sum-
> mary executions." . . . The same memo talks of a special commando
> unit, which carried out "abductions, bombings, street assassinations, and
> executions of real or alleged Communists." More than 25 years later, a
> CIA cable confirmed that civilian villages were targeted because of the
> [American-backed] army's belief that their Mayan Indian inhabitants
> were aiding the guerrillas. "Several villages have been burned to the
> ground," the cable tells Washington. [The commission] confirmed that
> entire communities were massacred. It said children were killed, ab-
> ducted, forcibly recruited as soldiers, illegally adopted, and sexually
> abused. Fetuses were cut from their mothers' wombs and young children
> were smashed against walls or thrown alive into pits. As late as April 1998
> Bishop Juan Gerardi, who coordinated the Catholic Church's report on
> atrocities, was brutally murdered.

For its part, the *New York Times* was not satisfied to restrict the record
of U.S.-sponsored atrocities to Guatemala alone. Commenting on President Clinton's tour in an editorial, the paper recalled an earlier visit by
President Ronald Reagan to the region in 1982—the "peak period," as the
Times instructed its readers, in Guatemala's military genocide of its Indian
communities. Just as bad, the paper continued, that period was marked by

President Reagan's incessant "praise of military leaders" in both Guatemala and El Salvador and by misguided policies that led us to "spen[d] billions in lethal aid to their governments and the Nicaraguan contras."

The tone of this and similar commentary throughout the world press may help explain why President Clinton felt obliged to address the matter as he did in the course of his tour. His words of apology cannot be lightly dismissed — even if they issue from a man who, as every American has had occasion to learn, habitually experiences no great difficulty apologizing for acts for which he feels no contrition. In a single sentence, the president of the United States finally said what our homegrown "peace constituency" and its epigones in the media had been dying to hear for decades: that in Central America, if not indeed elsewhere in the world during the cold war, the United States was on the "wrong side" of history.

It will be a long time before this latest exercise in historical revisionism is ever effectively countered by a firm appreciation of the facts, if for no other reason than that most Americans — including, it would seem, President Clinton himself — know precious little about Central America and are not interested in learning more. Nor do they or he seem to have much of a grasp of the history, even the quite recent history, of U.S. policy in each of the six greatly different republics that occupy the isthmus. But let us, in what follows, do what we can.

First, Guatemala. Even without the benefit of the Historical Clarification Commission and the documents recently declassified by the National Security Archive, no serious observer can gloss over the essentially tragic nature of that country's recent and not so recent past. Central America's most populous republic, it was in colonial times the seat of the Spanish captains-general; but for most of the time since its independence in 1821 it has been basically a feudal society, one whose large Indian majority (divided, however, into sixty language groups) has been exploited by cruel, ruthless "white" landowners eagerly assisted by ladino (mixed-race) politicians and military officers.

For most of this century, Guatemala was ruled by dictators, whether civilian or military. One of them, Manuel Estrada Cabrera (1898–1920) — the inspiration for *El Señor Presidente* (1946), a novel by the Nobel laureate Miguel Angel Asturias — was among the first Latin American authoritarians to create his own secret police. He also plundered the treasury, greatly expanded the standing army, and systematically jailed or exiled his opponents. His successor, Jorge Ubico (1931–44), was by some accounts even worse, though he ended debt peonage for the Indians and clamped down on corruption.

My excuse for dipping into this ancient history is that much of the commentary about Guatemala in today's press suggests, at least by indirection, that the country was a bucolic paradise before (to use the words of an Associated Press report) it was "split" apart by the "American-backed coup [that] put rightists in power in 1954." The truth is quite the contrary: Guatemalan society was "split" before, during, and after the regime of the ousted Jacobo Arbenz, who managed to add a few wrinkles of his own to his country's characteristic pathologies.

More history, not quite so ancient: Arbenz was a young military officer who had participated in Guatemala's revolution of 1944, an event that not only sent the dictator Ubico into exile but brought to power an entirely new generation of civilian and military leaders. The emblematic figure of that revolution was President Juan José Arévalo (ruled 1944–50), a somewhat otherworldly intellectual who considered himself a "spiritual socialist." Although not particularly radical, Arévalo was both weak and inept as an administrator and was inclined to turn a blind eye both to corruption and to communist infiltration of Guatemala's labor unions and educational system. Constitutional guarantees were suspended for roughly half the time he was in power.

One of those most disturbed by Arévalo's performance in office was Colonel Javier Arana, a hero of the revolution of 1944 who was assassinated under mysterious circumstances before the 1950 presidential elections. Although no conclusive evidence has ever linked him to this murder, Jacobo Arbenz was certainly its principal beneficiary, replacing Arana as defense minister and inheriting the latter's mantle of political succession. Arbenz's own victory in 1950 was assured by a combination of positive and negative sanctions: Government funds were used to bus Indians to polling places, and two prominent opposition candidates were conveniently exiled.

The Arbenz regime was notable for the emergence of the Guatemalan Communist Party as its principal prop. In return for the party's electoral support, the country's labor federation quickly came under communist domination, and a confiscatory land reform law was drafted that affected, among others, the United Fruit Company, the biggest landlord in Guatemala.[1] (When the law was declared unconstitutional by the supreme court, Arbenz ordered the removal of the court's offending members.) As for the opposition, it was kept at bay by the Civil Guard, which—while by no means as brutal as its successors—freely engaged in torture, murder, and intimidation.

By March 1954 Arbenz had unambiguously reaffirmed his support for the Guatemalan Communists, referring to them as the "democratic and progressive forces of the revolution." Meanwhile, he ordered 2,000 tons of weapons from Eastern Europe to arm a workers' and peasants' brigade. It was surely this action—a threat to any standing army—that precipitated his regime's terminal crisis. Although the CIA had organized a small insurrectionary force in neighboring Honduras, and engaged in some sophisticated political warfare, Arbenz was overthrown not by this small column of men but by his own armed forces at home.

With the advantage of hindsight, one can say that the United States might well have held back from involvement in Guatemala's domestic political turmoil. For one thing, Arbenz's primitive and dogmatic economic notions, combined with his disposition to ignore or repress his opposition—plus the vast liability represented by his close alliance with the Communists—might well have led in any case to his overthrow. For another, while the United States did not invent Guatemala's problems, by intervening in such a dramatic and obvious way, it acquired a kind of indirect responsibility for everything that happened thereafter. For still another, as the late CIA planner Richard Bissell wrote in his memoirs, *Reflections of a Cold Warrior* (1996), the celerity with which Arbenz was dislodged encouraged the entire national security establishment in Washington to overestimate the potential of covert warfare. "For many policy-

1. The United Fruit connection has produced a lush undergrowth of mythology, the purpose of which is to establish that U.S. hostility to Arbenz was fueled exclusively by corporate interests. In fact, as the case of Cuba was to show several years later, Washington was far more frightened by the prospect of communism than by punitive expropriations, which were after all nothing new.

makers outside the CIA," Bissell recalls, "it became a quick fix, an easy way to deal with hostile foreign leaders and renegade nation-states." A short and direct line runs from the overthrow of Arbenz to the Bay of Pigs disaster in 1961.

Still and all, it is not impossible that, left to its own devices, Guatemala might have become the first client-state of the Soviet Union in Latin America. To judge by Arbenz's trajectory after 1954 as a serial guest of Soviet-style police states in Prague and Havana, he might even have pre-ceded Fidel Castro in convincing the Kremlin to abandon its old habit of assigning Latin America to the U.S. sphere of influence. We will never know. But these were the concerns of the U.S. government and the Central Intelligence Agency at the time, and subsequent events in Cuba only five years later suggest that they were by no means frivolous or irresponsible.

Where Washington can be criticized most harshly is on the score of inattention; having seen the overthrow of Arbenz, it lost all interest in the quality of Guatemala's government under his successors. Even so, in con-sidering Guatemala after Arbenz it is necessary to parse a long stretch of time—from 1954 to 1991. First there were the purges under the regime of Colonel Carlos Castillo Armas (ruled 1954–60). Next came the devel-opment of an armed guerrilla movement with Cuban and Soviet assistance (1960–77). This was followed by a period of U.S. sanctions and an embargo on arms and training (1977–86). Fourth, and finally, Guatemala came to be governed by a sequence of elected governments (1986–91).

From the point of view of assessing U.S. complicity, the first and second periods were the worst. But of the two, the first, constituting the immediate post-Arbenz years from 1954 to 1960, seems almost benevolent compared with what came later, characterized more by garden-variety political persecution (leftist politicians and labor leaders forced to flee, leftist intellectuals dismissed from educational posts or other government jobs) than by mass murder. In those years, political conflict was largely centered in Guatemala's cities and did not involve the tactical military in a major way.

Things changed after the Cuban revolution in 1959–60, when Fidel Castro began to export a new form of revolution based on guerrilla warfare in the countryside. As in a number of other countries threatened by Cuban-sponsored insurgencies, the United States now became deeply involved

in training the Guatemalan army in counterinsurgency, a skill for which—
to say the least—it showed none of the requisite professional skill, patience,
or political imagination.

Why did the United States not disengage itself at this point? The
answer has partly to do with bureaucratic inertia, partly with the incurably
optimistic American conviction that foreign armies can be reshaped into
our own image and likeness. But the fundamental reason was that the cold
war in Latin America was then at its height, with Cuban and Soviet-
sponsored guerrilla movements operating in a dozen countries. Guatemala, as it happens, was one of the two key targets selected by Castro for
subversion (the other was Venezuela) and could not easily be abandoned
without important geopolitical consequences.

And the guerrilla challenge in Guatemala was by no means negligible.
For much of the 1960s, large parts of the countryside were controlled by
the Armed Revolutionary Forces (FAR), which on occasion showed themselves capable of reaching deep into the capital; in 1968, they managed to
assassinate the U.S. ambassador.

By the mid-1970s, this threat had receded to the point where Washington could afford the luxury of casting a skeptical eye on some of its
more unsavory allies. Important figures in the Ford administration—most
notably, Assistant Secretary of State William D. Rogers, as well as our
diplomatic representatives in Guatemala City and at the Inter-American
Commission on Human Rights—deliberately distanced themselves from
the regime. But the decisive change came with the Carter administration.
In 1977, the United States for the first time conditioned its military aid to
Guatemala on an improved human rights performance—a policy that
(under somewhat different circumstances) was extended well into the
second Reagan administration in the mid-1980s. In other words, from
1977 to 1986, in the third of the four periods under discussion, the United
States provided Guatemala with no military assistance, no foreign military
sales, and exactly $300,000 in training—and that only in 1985, after the
armed forces had agreed to return to their barracks.

The chronology here is crucial. First, it gives the lie to the claim of
the *New York Times* that the Reagan administration transferred "billions
in lethal aid" to the Guatemalan government. Second, as the report of the
Historical Clarification Commission also establishes, it was precisely when

U.S. influence in Guatemala was at its nadir that the vast majority of human rights violations —the "peak period," to revert to the *Times*'s misleading language—occurred in that country. (The article in the *Guardian* similarly obscures this point by collapsing events that occurred during that period with earlier moments.)

What was really going on? Throughout the long U.S. embargo—an embargo extending well beyond military aid to a proscription on ordinary development assistance—the Guatemalan government, then as usual run by the army, pointedly thumbed its nose at Washington and went its own way. It was able to do so in part because other countries, notably Spain, France, and Italy—even under socialist governments!—eagerly stepped forward to offer the training being denied by the United States.

The ironies here are multiple. By teaching the Guatemalan military just how easy and painless it was to flout Washington, the American embargo strengthened the hand of the most vicious and intransigent officers and their allies in the business community and removed whatever restraints might have been inhibiting them from fighting the civil war on their own terms and in their own way. To put matters baldly, these people preferred to be liberated from U.S. interference and, during the 1980s, often bragged that, unlike their counterparts in El Salvador, they had not "sold out" to the Yankees. (One of Washington's major concerns during this period was, in fact, that the example of Guatemala's "independence" would prove too attractive to the farthest right in El Salvador and its potential allies in the armed forces.)

To be sure, even when the United States was not actively engaged in Guatemala, it continued to maintain an intelligence presence there, as it did in scores of other countries. This explains why so many U.S. government documents utilized by the Historical Clarification Commission could be so exact in their recounting of army atrocities. To the *Washington Post*'s correspondent, this fact bears a sinister significance: Because we knew about these things, presumably we approved of them. But the sad truth is that there was no point in making representations to a military institution over which we had absolutely no leverage.

In retrospect, perhaps a loud and direct denunciation in some public forum—say, the United Nations Human Rights Commission—would have served our own national purposes better. I for one certainly think so.

But let no one be deceived: It would not have moved the Guatemalan military one millimeter in the right direction.

Before his visit to Guatemala, President Clinton stopped off in El Salvador. In the foreign policy debates of the 1980s, this country loomed almost as large in the American consciousness as China. Its civil war, we were repeatedly told by the guardians of the liberal conscience, gave us only two alternatives: entering into peace negotiations with the Marxist guerrillas organized in the Farabundo Marti National Liberation Front (FMLN), who had earned the right to rule their country, or abetting certain genocide by the government-sponsored military and death squads — in effect, another Guatemala.

In the event, neither happened. The Reagan administration persisted in supporting an elected civilian government as well as military operations to contain and defeat the insurgency. This policy exacted a considerable human cost, but El Salvador today is blessed by a degree of civic peace and institutional normality unprecedented in its history. It is also experiencing high rates of economic growth. The guerrillas are now in the unicameral National Assembly, where they vote and sit on committees. If this is not a policy success, one wonders what would be.

In light of what has happened in El Salvador since the end of the war, it is especially interesting to recall the debates of the 1980s. The implicit and sometimes explicit assumption of critics of the Reagan administration — in Congress and the media, in the churches and the human rights community — was that, in reluctantly taking up arms, the FMLN guerrillas embodied the desires of the repressed majority of the country. Now the dirty little secret can be told, and, to the discomfiture of the critics, it turns out to be just the opposite. The repressed majority of the country wanted a government not of the FMLN but of the nationalist right, whose emblematic figure was the late Roberto d'Aubuisson, a founder of the ARENA party and shady eminence of the death squads.

So much was this the will of the people of El Salvador that, in 1984, the CIA was forced to rig elections there in order to permit José Napoleon Duarte, a candidate minimally acceptable to U.S. congressional Democrats, to win the presidency; anything else would have led to a vote in Washington cutting off military and economic aid. Similarly, the Reagan administration was forced into uncharacteristic adventures like land reform in order to prove—less to the Salvadoran peasants than to Catholic bishops in the United States—that in opposing Marxism in El Salvador we were not trying simply to shore up the socioeconomic status quo.

Today, although d'Abuisson has long since died, he remains a legendary if politically irrelevant presence in El Salvador, and his party continues to win consecutive presidential elections. Meanwhile, the FMLN, running unimpeded under its own banners, has consistently failed to garner as much as 30 percent of the vote (though it has managed to capture the city hall in San Salvador, the capital, and some provincial mayorships).

This sort of thing takes a lot of explaining away. In the most recent presidential election, which more or less coincided with President Clinton's visit, the correspondent of the *New York Times*, forced to report on the eve of voting that the ARENA candidate was running ahead in the polls, tried to minimize the fact by emphasizing how low the turnout rate was expected to be, thus presumably demonstrating the growing political alienation of ordinary El Salvadorans. To make the point more directly, the *Times* reporter conscripted Reverend José Maria Tojeira, rector of the Central American University, to say that while "ARENA is more moderate [now] than in d'Aubuisson's day, . . . it's in the hands of rich people who don't favor social change." The next day, 52 percent of the voters cast their ballots for ARENA's candidate, a thirty-nine-year-old academic named Francisco Flores. Even with a reduced voter turnout (in fact the turnout ran between 40 and 50 percent of the electorate), there is no way this number can be construed to represent only or even principally "rich people who don't favor social change."

After the election, readers of the *Times* were told hopefully that the "democratic transformation" of El Salvador would have been "even more remarkable if the FMLN . . . had been able to build on previous electoral victories"—that is, in plain English, if it had managed to do better than 29 percent in the presidential race. But if the test of a country's "democratic transformation" is the specific electoral outcome favored by the *Times*, then El Salvador, along with dozens of other countries, may never arrive at its destination. In fact, it is the participation of the Front in the electoral process and local government—as opposed to its former preference for terror, kidnapping, and political assassination—that speaks most eloquently to the quality of the country's "democratic transformation."

But one must not be too hard on the *Times*. Even in the most earnest precincts of "progressive" journalism, a few inconvenient facts do manage to creep in at the margins. Thus, in a profile of the president-elect, we were informed that Francisco Flores had decided to enter politics only when the Marxist guerrillas killed his father-in-law, who in the late 1980s had served as chief of staff to the democratically elected President Federico Cristiani. In the same article it also emerged that, for his part, the candidate of the FMLN, one Francisco Guardado, had been unable to allay widespread popular apprehensions in El Salvador with regard to the past activities of his movement; in effect, Guardado "could not overcome aversions to a Left remembered in El Salvador as violent and destructive." Just why the left should be so remembered in El Salvador was something that readers of the *Times* were tactfully left to puzzle out on their own.

On his March tour of the area, President Clinton also called at Honduras and Nicaragua. Press coverage of those stops focused mainly on the damage from Hurricane Mitch—the ostensible occasion for Clinton's visit—as well as on the role of U.S. active and reserve forces in helping stricken inhabitants reconstruct their shattered lives. Still, considering the media's lurid preoccupation with the seamy details of life under previous right-wing regimes in Guatemala and El Salvador, it might seem curious that no one was interested in revisiting the recent political history of Nicaragua and the role of U.S. policy there. But perhaps it is not so curious after all.

In the late 1970s, thanks in no small part to the maladroit policies of the Carter administration, Nicaragua, with hardly a pause for breath, went straight from an old-fashioned dictatorship of the right under the Somoza dynasty to a more "modern" dictatorship of the Marxist-Leninist left—the Sandinista Front. By the time Ronald Reagan assumed the American presidency in January 1981, the country was flooded with Cuban, Bulgarian, and East German "economists," political commissars, and specialists in police, intelligence, and military matters, and the regime boasted an army and police force bigger than that of its predecessor by several orders of magnitude. Moderate members of the original anti-Somoza junta had long since been pushed out of power by the Communists and were living under the threat of mob violence and worse.

None of this, however, fazed liberal Democrats in the U.S. Congress or their allies in the media, who reserved their indignation for the local opponents of the newly installed Sandinista government, tarring them with the *somocista* brush. This tactic enjoyed a broad measure of plausibility in 1981 and 1982, when most of the armed Nicaraguan opposition to the Sandinistas was indeed concentrated among former officers of the disbanded National Guard, who were operating from bases in Honduras with the counsel and assistance of officers dispatched from the Argentine military dictatorship (and, it was subsequently revealed, with active assistance from the CIA).

By 1983, however, the anti-Sandinista movement had grown into a genuinely popular national cause—far more popular, in fact, than the cause of the Sandinistas themselves had ever been. Yet the anticommunist partisans (contras) who appeared more or less by spontaneous generation in Nicaragua were immediately denounced in this country as "rightists" and worse. As Robert S. Leiken shows in his forthcoming study of the period, *A Picture Held Us Captive: Nicaragua in the American Imagination*, no anticommunist insurgency in history—including the rebel movement in Afghanistan—ever received such negative treatment in the American press, particularly in television news. And as for the U.S. Congress, during the second Reagan administration (1985–89), the near-totality of Democratic effort in Central America was aimed at ending U.S. support for the contras—which is to say, at rescuing the Sandinistas from the consequences of their own tyrannical misrule.

Just why so many Democratic members of Congress were so active in the anti-anti-Sandinista campaign is difficult to say. Few, surely, were sympathetic to Marxism in any form. Many may have felt that, having propped up the Somoza regime for so many years (in fact, American support had been spotty and, by the mid to late 1970s, had veered from encouragement of Somoza to outright hostility), the United States "owed" it to the Nicaraguan people to give any successor regime the benefit of the doubt. As in the case of El Salvador, there was also an unconscious and quite false assumption that the vast majority of Nicaraguans were leftists of some sort or other. When it came to Nicaragua, many Americans appeared to believe that the test of any authentic and truly representative government was not whether it had been elected by popular vote, or even whether it was good or bad for Nicaraguans, much less whether it was allied with Cuba and the Soviet Union, but rather the degree to which it was anti-American. On that score, at least, the Sandinistas passed with flying colors.

All this would be put to the test in 1990. In that year, the Sandinistas, apparently believing the propaganda of their admirers in the United States and Western Europe, chose to fall into the trap of holding presidential elections. So sure were they of victory that their supporters around the world flooded American embassies with letters demanding that we "respect the results of the Nicaraguan elections." The outcome—a smashing victory for the anti-Sandinista forces led by Violeta Chamorro over Sandinista president Daniel Ortega—was quite possibly the most devastating ideological defeat the Western intellectual left has ever experienced.

Clearly, this was not the result we had been asked to "respect." Nor did the Sandinistas themselves respect it. Once ejected by popular vote, they rushed with indecent haste to "privatize" the vast property holdings they had confiscated after 1979, with themselves as the beneficiaries. But not even this looting expedition—a huge piñata, as it was called—was enough to unmask them once and for all in the eyes of their well-wishers. Immediately after the elections of 1990, former president Jimmy Carter rushed to Violeta Chamorro's house in the capital city of Managua to urge her, in the name of "national reconciliation," to retain for the Sandinistas a measure of power in the new government. She graciously, but mistakenly, concurred; until recently, the Nicaraguan army remained the Sandinista army, and its commander, General Humberto Ortega, was the same man who had commanded it in the 1980s. The result has been truly lamentable: neither genuine national reconciliation nor, thanks largely to unresolved claims to expropriated property, a serious recovery of Nicaragua's economy.

Since the United States is in a forgiveness-begging mood these days, one is almost tempted to suggest that former president Carter personally ask the pardon of the Nicaraguan people for his two-decade-long role in bringing about their present plight—first by quickening Somoza's hopes in the late 1970s that he could somehow remain in power, then by imposing an arms embargo that made it impossible to persuade the National Guard to eject Somoza when the dictator entered his political death agonies a short time later, finally by rushing back to the country to save the Sandinistas' bacon (or what was left of it) after they had been roundly defeated at the ballot box. As long as contrition is the new national style, ought we not spread it around?

There are many people today in Washington and elsewhere who sincerely believe that the Soviet Union was never a threat during the cold war, and that, in opposing it, the United States was uselessly wasting time and resources. For such people, there was no danger of Sovietization, much less of Cubanization, in Central America and U.S. efforts to combat this danger were unjustified if not wholly delusory.

Most Americans, however, did not believe this at the time and do not believe it now. For them, the problem was how best to face the Soviet-Cuban challenge. Without question, in some countries we faced it more deftly, more humanely, and more intelligently than in others. But our success or failure was determined as much by local conditions and the allies we were able to find as it was by our own perspicacity or lack of it. Central America was certainly one of the more morally difficult venues in which to fight the cold war, for the task there was not only to defeat Communists and their allies but to help construct a civic order qualitatively better than anything in the past.

In setting about that latter task, we did not achieve miracles. But no one looking with an unprejudiced eye can deny that the region today is far better off than it has ever been before and that it is assuredly far better off than it would have been with Marxist guerrillas in power in Guatemala, El Salvador, and Nicaragua. On that score, at least, there is no cause for regret or apology, nor should any be offered.

COLD WAR

PART TWO
Op-Eds and
Brief Articles

1

Cold Water and Cold War Triumphalism

Arnold Beichman

Arnold Beichman, a research fellow at the Hoover Institution, Stanford University, is coauthor of *Yuri Andropov: New Challenge to the West*, author of *The Long Pretense: Soviet Treaty Diplomacy from Lenin to Gorbachev*, and a columnist for the *Washington Times*. This article first appeared in the *Washington Times*, January 4, 1998. Copyright 1998 News World Communications, Inc. Reprinted with permission of the *Washington Times*.

Sometime next fall, the world will be favored by a twenty-four-part television history of the cold war. Since its patron is Ted Turner, the billionaire superliberal of liberals, I will predict the $15 million film will follow two themes of mainstream academic historical writing: (1) the overriding anti-American theme that nobody won the cold war (a recent article in the *Chronicle of Higher Education* was titled "The United States Was the Loser in the Cold War"); (2) the cold war as America fought it was an undemocratic aberration.

The Turner film will document something the great Austrian economist Joseph Schumpeter once said: "Selective information, if in itself correct, is an attempt to lie by speaking the truth."

How can I possibly know this when the film isn't even in the can, when yards and yards of film are probably still lying around on the cutting room floor in an office in London's Leicester Square? I offer as evidence a startling paragraph from a *New York Times* interview in London quoting Sir Jeremy Isaacs, its executive producer, about Turner 's vision of the project: "He [Turner] wanted a project that dealt unjingoistically with the Cold War. He did not want a triumphalist approach."

That second sentence — "He did not want a triumphalist approach" — and the adverb "unjingoistically" tell me all I need to know about what Mr. Turner intends with this film: to show, first, that the United States was as much at fault as the Soviet Union if not more so, in starting the cold war and, second, that Ronald Reagan's leadership had nothing to do with winning the cold war since Russia was already weak and harmless. (Robert Conquest has dealt with the "harmless enemy" fallacy with his mordant observation that one need not worry about a rabid dog since he's going to die anyway.)

In fact, triumphalism is a neologism used by liberals to revile those who tell the historical truth about communist totalitarianism. Triumphalism is the slur word that has for liberals replaced "red-baiting" as a term of reproach.

Mr. Turner is reported as admiring two World War II documentaries, the twenty-six-part British series, *World at War*, and the American *Victory at Sea*. These documentaries were, of course, "triumphalist" in tone and content. How could they not be, dealing as they did with victory over a depraved Japanese empire (remember the Bataan death march, the "comfort women," and the earlier rape of Nanking) and an even greater victory over the Hitlerite fascist empire, whose cruelties and barbarism were only to be equaled and then exceeded by the Lenin-Stalin years of the Soviet empire?

Mr. Turner had told the producer, according to Sir Jeffrey, that he didn't want the documentary's approach to the cold war to be either that of the Soviet Union or of the United States. Can you imagine producing a documentary on the end of apartheid and the rise of Nelson Mandela in a nontriumphalist, above-the-battle approach? Nobody suggested that the editorial approach of the two documentaries Mr. Turner so admired — *World at War* and *Victory at Sea* — should not be either that of the Allies or that of Nazi Germany. But it is only when you might accurately depict the fall of the Soviet Union as the triumph of the human spirit over oppression, the triumph of freedom over the fictions of Marxism-Leninism that the censorious cries of "triumphalism" and "jingoism" are heard.

Mr. Turner's view of the last days of the Soviet Union can be judged by his statement in 1990: "Gorbachev has probably moved more quickly than any person in the history of the world. Moving faster than Jesus Christ did. America is always lagging six months behind." Christ was a laggard?

The *New York Times* quotes Mr. Turner as saying that President Reagan's use of the phrase "evil empire" to describe the USSR was frightening. Yet, according to David Remnick, for some Russians, Mr. Reagan became a hero. "He called us the 'Evil Empire,'" Arkady Murashev, a leader of Democratic Russia close to Boris Yeltsin, told Mr. Remnick in 1991. "So why did you in the West laugh at him? It's true!" Mr. Murashev was then chief of the Moscow police department. Andrei Kozyrev, Russia's then foreign minister, was quoted in the March 15, 1992, *Los Angeles Times* as saying, "the Soviet Union had really been an evil empire." He compared the "mass crimes" under the Soviet dictatorship to the revelations about the Nazis at the Nuremberg trials. Perhaps Mr. Turner's researchers have interviewed Messrs. Murashev and Kozyrev, or if they haven't they will now. I hope and pray that everything I have predicted in the foregoing paragraphs about the Turner cold war epic will be proved wrong in each and every particular.

2

Ted's Reds

Arnold Beichman

Arnold Beichman, a research fellow at the Hoover Institution, Stanford University, is coauthor of *Yuri Andropov: New Challenge to the West*, author of *The Long Pretense: Soviet Treaty Diplomacy from Lenin to Gorbachev*, and a columnist for the *Washington Times*. This article first appeared in the *Weekly Standard* 4, no. 8 (November 2, 1998): 36–39.

Ted Turner's new, $12 million weekly CNN series on the cold war—whose first episode aired on September 27, 1998, and which continues every Sunday until April 19, 1999—is not without merit. Yet as I previewed the twenty-four episodes, fifty minutes each, I was reminded of the timid young English curate who, having been invited to his first breakfast with the bishop, was served with a rotten egg. When his ecclesiastical host inquired of the curate how he had found his meal, the curate replied, "Parts of it were excellent, Your Grace."

Parts of the Turner extravaganza are excellent, and parts of it are dreary beyond measure—especially the long sermons on Marxism-Leninism by Turner's personal friend and duck-hunting companion Fidel Castro. No one would dare impose on an audience such Castrovian drivel unless driven by his financial backer, which is what must have happened to the series' producer, Sir Jeremy Isaacs. Just when you think you've seen the last of him, there Castro is again ranting away to the invisible interviewer. Did it not occur to Isaacs to add an interview or two with Armando Valladares or any other of the thousands of Fidel's victims?

The great virtue of Turner's film is that it brings to life some of the history we have lived through. It shows much dramatic footage: the capture, trial, and execution of the Ceauşescus in Romania on Christmas Day 1989; scenes from the June 17, 1953, uprising in Berlin; the 1956 revolts in Poland and Hungary; the 1968 occupation of Czechoslovakia; the Stalinist trials in Eastern Europe. The filmmakers found a Russian woman in Soviet intelligence who confirmed that Roosevelt's Soviet-owned villa at Tehran was bugged and transcripts of the American discussions were delivered each morning to Stalin's dacha.

Of course, no film based on oral interviews can ever be real history in the way in which great historians write history. Oral history usually suffers from faulty memory and the narrator's desire to give—as the Grand Pooh-Bah put it in *The Mikado*—"artistic verisimilitude to an otherwise bald and unconvincing narrative."

And yet, though a television program intended for popular consumption can't be a historical monograph, the conscientious (as opposed to the tendentious) historian will test his findings against all available evidence. And that's exactly what Turner's CNN series never manages to do.

This is not to say that CNN's scriptwriters falsify the now obvious in Soviet history. After all, Nikita Khrushchev denounced Stalin in 1956. So Stalin, we are told and shown, was a tyrant who murdered millions of peasants, instituted a reign of terror, and established a police state.

What the film doesn't do (and perhaps movie documentaries cannot do) is present an explanation of why, once the totalitarian system was installed, the cold war became inevitable. Former Soviet foreign minister Alexander Bessmertnykh has argued that the cold war started not with Churchill's "Iron Curtain" speech in Fulton, Missouri, on March 5, 1946, but rather three decades earlier with the Bolshevik revolution. Totalitarianism—the unrestrained rule by terror and modern technology, the destroyer of civil society and law, the society in which no one was innocent—was a new social force, said Hannah Arendt, radically different from the tyrannies and dictatorships of the past.

But if the failure of Turner's extravaganza to capture the international aspects of the cold war derives from the general inability of the film to present that sort of history, the CNN series fails as well where it might have succeeded: in presenting the domestic aspects of the cold war. It is with McCarthyism and Vietnam that Turner's anti-anticommunism and claim of "moral equivalence" shows itself most glaringly and where producer Isaacs himself demonstrates a lack of understanding.

You can't go wrong showing Joe McCarthy—his "five o'clock shadow," his half-whinning, half-droning voice—but is that all there was to it? Turner's series juxtaposes the McCarthy era with the Soviet Gulag. Were there no anti-Communists with impeccable civil rights records who might have been interviewed? CNN might have quoted Diana Trilling, who wrote that "a staunch anti-Communism was the great moral-political imperative of our epoch." Or the seminal writings of Sidney Hook, who described McCarthyism as "cultural vigilantism." Or there might have been a filmed reference to the liberal journalist Nicholas von Hoffman, who wrote in the *Washington Post* in 1996 that "enough new information has come to light about the Communists in the U.S. government that we may now say that point by point Joe McCarthy got it all wrong and yet was still closer to the truth than those who ridiculed him." J. Robert Oppenheimer is in the film but not his nemesis, Edward Teller.

Although there is no room in the twenty-four episodes for anticommunist intellectuals, there is lots of room and sympathy for Paul Robeson, winner of the Stalin Peace Prize in 1952. Robeson sang at rallies to protest aid to Britain, when it stood alone against the Nazis. In 1948, Robeson supported the communist-controlled Progressive Party and its willing dupe, Henry A. Wallace. "Robeson went around the world," as Professor William O'Neill put it, "endorsing a political system based on mass murder, forced labor and the denial of every human right, accusing all who criticized him for doing so of bigotry."

One of the CNN episodes, entitled "Make Love Not War," deals with the street battle in Chicago at the 1968 Democratic convention and the SDS in the late 1960s and 1970s. The writer of this episode is Germaine Greer, a woman deeply implicated in the domestic battles of those days. Why not a moment to discuss Norman Podhoretz's *Why We Were in Vietnam*, which demolishes incredible statements by Greer's sisters Mary McCarthy, Susan Sontag, and Frances Fitzgerald? Or Guenter Lewy's *America in Vietnam?* Or Paul Hollander's *Political Pilgrims: Western Intellectuals in Search of the Good Society?*

The series is at its worst in its selection of Soviet apologists, who are allowed to spout forth all kinds of nonsense without refutation. Soviet general Nikolai Detinov explains that the outcry when the Soviet Union pointed its new SS-20 missiles westward was unjustified because "no one had any plans to attack Europe using SS-20s." Is it possible that Turner's researchers overlooked Richard Pipes's famous 1979 *Commentary* report, which, citing article after article in Soviet military journals, showed that the Soviet Union believed it could fight and win a nuclear war?

Lavrenti Beria's son, Sergio, reports that he heard Stalin tell his father that the reason for the Stalin-Hitler pact, signed in August 1939, was that the Soviet Union needed two years to prepare for the inevitable war with Nazi Germany. Was there no one to explain to CNN that Stalin did everything he could to strengthen Hitler right up to the very June 1941 day of the Nazi invasion, when Soviet freight cars loaded with war essentials were traveling to Germany? Communist parties in the West, uttering obscene cries that fighting fascism was an imperialist plot, sabotaged the resistance of embattled France and Britain. In the United States the Communists in 1940 called political strikes to prevent France from receiving fighter planes it had paid for, and they cheered Hitler when France fell in June 1940. Stalin welcomed every Nazi victory. The CNN interviewers let the son of the monster Beria get away with his defense of the Stalin-Hitler pact.

A CIA officer, Paul Henze, does receive a short interview, but he is never asked about his expertise on an event that goes unmentioned in the film: the attempted assassination of Pope John Paul II on May 13, 1981, in St. Peter's Square. The destruction of Korean Airlines flight 007 on September 1, 1983, however, is treated fairly, with a fascinating interview with the Soviet pilot who, following orders, shot down the passenger plane.

American foreign policy in Central and South America throughout the cold war is dealt with at great length, and everything that the United States did there is declared wrong. Wouldn't it have been of some interest to have sought out Elliot Abrams, onetime assistant secretary of state for Central America, and to have asked him what he thought of the Soviet spokesman's claim of a hands-off policy towards Guatemala's Communist Party?

Fidel Castro is the star of this Turner production, with his only rival the onetime president of the USSR, Mikhail Gorbachev—the man of whom Ted Turner once told *Time* magazine, "Gorbachev has probably moved more quickly than any person in the history of the world. Moving faster than Jesus Christ did." Turner's researchers overlook some of Gorbachev's more questionable statements made during his *offensive du charme* while he was running the USSR. "Stalinism is a concept thought up by the enemies of communism to discredit socialism as a whole," he told an interviewer in 1986. As late as 1990, he said: "I am a Communist, a convinced Communist. For some that may be a fantasy, but for me, it is my main goal."

One of the more striking omissions from the series is the USSR's signal failure over seventy years to lure Western and Asian trade unions into its orbit. Despite the Kremlin's enormous expenditures, the AFL-CIO, the British Trades Union Congress, and the German DGB remained opposed to Moscow. Omitted also in what is otherwise an inspiring episode in the CNN series—the Berlin airlift—is the role of organized labor. General Lucius D. Clay, U.S. commander in Germany, attested to labor's contribution in unloading and distributing the two and a half million tons of food, coal, and other supplies delivered day and night between June 1948 and May 1949.

The most serious failure of this cold war series it that it doesn't ask the question why we didn't have a cold war with Britain, France, or any other country. I do not believe that it is simply because the Kremlin wanted to rule the world, although it did. The cold war was the outgrowth of the deliberate misunderstanding of Soviet aims and the pretending by Churchill and Roosevelt during World War II that the Soviet Union could be a trustworthy postwar ally and in time become a democratic society. Nothing else explains FDR's foolish statement in 1945 about the genocidal Stalin: "I think that if I give him everything I possibly can without demanding anything in return, then, *noblesse oblige*, he will not attempt to annex anything and will work to build a peaceful and democratic world."

Churchill is shown making his "Iron Curtain" speech denouncing the Soviet empire. Forgotten is the day—February 27, 1945—when he told the House of Commons: "I know of no Government which stands to its obligations, even in its own despite, more solidly than the Russian Soviet government." And this at a time, as the CNN series shows, when the Red Army encamped on the banks of the Vistula while Polish freedom-fighters, emboldened by a promise of Soviet military support, attempted to retake Warsaw and were annihilated by the Reichswehr. Turner's cold war series shows footage of the 1940 murder of fifteen thousand Polish officers near Smolensk—but makes only a glancing reference to the fact that Churchill and Roosevelt, knowing that Stalin was responsible, said nothing when the Russians blamed the killing on the Nazis.

Similarly, the series makes reference to President Roosevelt's desire to recognize the Soviet Union as soon as he took office in 1933. There is no mention of the pleas from State Department advisers like Loy Henderson, Charles Bohlen, and even George Kennan to be cautious in negotiating recognition. As late as 1953, Kennan wrote that America "should never have established de jure relations with the Soviet government."

In dealing with the Rosenbergs, the Turner researchers missed Vyacheslav Molotov's confirmation that the Rosenbergs had indeed been atomic spies. In his six-hundred-page volume of oral reminiscences, Molotov says, "It cannot be ruled out that they helped us. But we should not talk about that. This might prove useful to us in the future." Oral history, of course, but we have the documents, the archives, the public trial to confirm Molotov.

Why all this hullabloo about a television series? Because Ted Turner, the billionaire ideologist, is going to peddle this documentary to schools at $230 for a set of twelve videos, two episodes on each one. This will be what our children learn about the cold war. They will learn moral equivalence: The Communists shoot students in Tiananmen Square, we shoot them at Kent State. They will see a few shots of such realists as Zbigniew Brzezinski and Condoleezza Rice, but many more of the likes of the historian Raymond Garthoff—the man who wrote in his book *The Great Transition*, "A Manichean communist worldview spawned a Manichean anticommunist worldview."

I am not suggesting that CNN is part of a vast left-wing conspiracy to brainwash our children or the American people about what happened during the cold war and why the cold war happened at all. I am suggesting something much worse—the full-flowering of a passé moral equivalence ideology that benefits from a technique once described by Joseph Schumpeter: "Selective information, if in itself correct, is an attempt to lie by speaking the truth."

3

Fractured Cold War Reflections

Arnold Beichman

Arnold Beichman, a research fellow at the Hoover Institution, Stanford University, is coauthor of *Yuri Andropov: New Challenge to the West*, author of *The Long Pretense: Soviet Treaty Diplomacy from Lenin to Gorbachev*, and a columnist for the *Washington Times*. This article first appeared in the *Washington Times*, February 25, 1999. Copyright © 1999, News World Communications, Inc. Reprinted with permission of the *Washington Times*.

This was the scholarly verdict pronounced in 1995 by Professor John Lewis Gaddis in his book *The United States and the End of the Cold War*: "To the astonishment of [President Reagan's] own hard-line supporters, what appeared to be an enthusiastic return to the Cold War in fact turned out to be a more solidly based approach to détente than anything that the Nixon, Ford or Carter administrations had been able to accomplish. . . .

"The last thing one would have anticipated at the time Ronald Reagan took office in 1981 was that he would use his eight years in the White House to bring about the most significant improvement in Soviet-American relations since the end of World War II. . . . [T]o see the president's policies solely in terms of his rhetoric, it is now clear, would have been quite wrong."

Four years later, this same distinguished historian lent his name to Ted Turner's caricature TV history of the cold war and an accompanying CNN textbook now being distributed among American public schools. The Turner-Gaddis episodes, which run weekly on CNN, make President Reagan out to be an ignoramus in foreign affairs and a feeble-minded scoundrel who concocted a "simplistic vision of an ideological crusade against communism." President Harry Truman is another scoundrel. The only American who is given heroic stature is Henry A. Wallace, onetime vice-president under President Roosevelt. Until 1950, Wallace was Josef Stalin's puppet.

One can expect such "history" from Ted Turner's CNN. After all, Ted Turner is the man who, when then Soviet president Mikhail Gorbachev was trying to revive the communist corpse, said in 1990: "Gorbachev has probably moved more quickly than any person in the history of the world. Moving faster than Jesus Christ did. America is always lagging six months behind." But one must ask how can a distinguished historian like Mr. Gaddis reconcile his adulatory 1995 opinions about Mr. Reagan's leadership with what he seems to believe today? This is something I leave to Professor Gaddis's conscience.

The CNN series has been attacked by, among others, Charles Krauthammer in the *Washington Post*, Jacob Heilbrun in the *New Republic*, Joseph Shattan in the *American Spectator*, and this writer in the *Weekly Standard*. Probably the most devastating analysis to date of CNN's corrupted history is to be found in the April 1999 issue of *Commentary* magazine under the title "Twenty-four Lies about the Cold War," a word play on the twenty-four film episodes of the Turner documentary.

After a lie-by-lie examination of the film, the analyst, Gabriel Schoenfeld, the magazine's senior editor, concludes that, as the CNN version of history proceeds, "the 'noble cause' of defending freedom is mocked, good is turned into evil and evil into good, and the moral and political categories that distinguish a democratic country like the United States from a totalitarian one like the USSR are blurred and then erased."

Ted Turner has produced a film and a book that are travesties of the history of the cold war. He has done so because of an aversion to democratic society in general and to the United States in particular and, above all, because of his obvious aversion to Ronald Reagan. The angry Turner focus on President Reagan as "villain" ironically confirms the fact that had it not been for this contemptible Hollywood movie actor, as Mr. Turner might put it, there would still be a Soviet empire and a regnant communism. Mr. Reagan was the first president to challenge the once extant idea that communist victories were irreversible and to act on that challenge with his "Star Wars" and his arms and missile buildup.

Mr. Turner's cold war series and textbook are being introduced into the standard curriculum of American high schools, according to the *Commentary* article. Our children are being exposed to a history that is not a history, a villainous president who was not a villain, and a duped American people who were not duped. Worst of all, our children will be taught not that with the end of the Soviet empire we live in a better world but rather that we live in a meaner world.

For is not Ted Turner's message really that we are all worse off because there no longer is a Soviet Union and that to have triumphed over that totalitarian empire was nothing short of a crime? Perhaps Professor Gaddis has an answer to that question.

4

History in the Making

Sir Jeremy Isaacs

Jeremy Isaacs was executive producer on *Cold War*. He and Taylor Downing wrote the accompanying book. This article first appeared in the *Guardian*, September 7, 1998.

When Ted Turner asked me in late 1994 to make *Cold War*, it was easy to agree in principle. Easy because the period to be covered, 1945 to 1991, was one we both lived through; easy because what he asked was what I wanted to do. Ted Turner is a remarkable figure in world media, an owner who cares about program content. He told his colleagues what he wanted in St. Petersburg during his 1994 Goodwill Games (Turner's antidote to the superpower rivalry that had wrecked the 1980 and 1984 Olympics). *Cold War* would be made to his broad specification and funded. "Go and get that Jeremy Irons who made *The World at War*," he said. I don't look like Jeremy Irons, but they tracked me down.

Turner wanted to tell a universal, not a partisan, story and to do justice to the experience, reasoning, motives, and actions of both the protagonist great powers involved—the United States and the Soviet Union—and of other countries also. And he and I both wanted to tell the story simply and directly, without gloss or spin, in visual images of record and through the memories and testimony of eyewitnesses to history.

This was the technique of *The World at War*, a history of World War II, which I made in the 1970s, of which Ted was a fan. But *Cold War* would be trickier and more complex; its spread was at least as wide; its duration much longer. The first critical decision was to present *Cold War* as a story. Television history is popular history: short on analysis, long on anecdote, big on the human incident that brings large political matters home. The trick is to keep a clear narrative going and resist the temptation to stray all over the place. We have (mostly) avoided thematic episodes that span the entire period of forty-five-plus years and instead arranged our subject matter so that each film, which is intended to stand on its own, follows from last week's episode and leads to the next. Thus, we hope to keep viewers on the edge of their seats, hungry for more, over a six-month span.

The blockbuster series is rare and getting rarer; one reason is that a head of documentaries who commissions a twenty-part series denies himself other choices. A channel controller, with an eye to the schedule, can give the go-ahead but only if he can afford it. Turner could decide to commission and to meet the cost. He did not hesitate. He knew what he wanted and went for it. Four months after our initial meeting—four months of lively London discussion as to how to proceed—we submitted a developed proposal and the answer came back from Atlanta in ten days flat: a green light.

Commitment to our next series, *Millennium*, came even more quickly, over an Easter weekend. Nobody in British television behaves like that these days, though once they did. Howard Thomas and Brian Tesler took only forty-eight hours to say yes to *The World at War*, after the government altered the basis of the ITV levy from revenue to profit and challenged them to spend the benefits on quality programs.

Because CNN footed the bill, BBC TV—Michael Jackson made the decision—has been able to acquire a run rather than commission the whole. CNN and I warmly welcome their involvement—the overseers from news (Tim Gardam and Mark Damazer) give the best viewing notes I have heard. But the decision that counted came from Georgia. From overseas program sales and on-air sponsorship the series is already in the black, with reruns and video sales to come. The new "commercial" BBC will readily recognize that returns accrue to the investor; you *can* do well by doing good.

The practicalities of my involvement in *Cold War* were another matter. At the time, I was general director of the Royal Opera House, where it was agreed I could be involved in one major outside project. *Cold War's* making would extend long past my time there, but there was no way I could fulfill the same role as I had done on *World at War*; there are simply not enough days in the week. Someone else would be series producer. The ideal candidate was at hand, Martin Smith.

He has driven it through to completion and held it all together. I have been there to back him up and, with my coexecutive producer (Pat Mitchell, president of CNN/Time Productions), have occasionally pointed the way. But neither the three of us together, nor any one of us, could have made *Cold War*. It was inevitably a team effort: an individual producer and writer for each episode and the best researchers in the world to find film and interviewees.

Svetlana Palmer, for example, had to browbeat ex-KGB generals into answering our questions. She tells how, on a Moscow building site, with a bottle of vodka to ease them through the night, she persuaded one Russian Afghan war veteran to talk of Soviet atrocities there and his nightmares afterward—Afghanistan as the USSR's Vietnam.

Cold War is intended to be more than sensation and to present a guide you can trust to the story of our time. Therefore, at every stage, we have had guidance from historians—American, Russian, British, and others—to keep us to the ascertainable truth. John Gaddis, Vlad Zubok, and Lawrence Freedman commented on every outline, every rough cut, every final script. We checked testimony and fact against a valid source and an objective record. *Cold War* could not possibly be the whole truth; in short television hours, we leave out a great deal. But it is as accurate as we can make it. This was not an assignment for a producer on an ego trip. It is responsibility to the facts—and to the audience—that counts.

In *Cold War*, world leaders speak: Bush, Gorbachev, Castro, and dozens more. But most people we talked to were not decision makers, just men and women affected by decisions the statesmen took, who lived the cold war and played their part in it: German women raped by Russians; Russian women who survived the Gulag; American women who lost their jobs in McCarthyite hysteria; women who fought in Angola or who saw killing in Nicaragua. Telling their stories to us are astronauts and spies, policemen and prisoners, farmers, priests, nurses; politicians and protesters in Berlin, Prague, Havana, Budapest, London, Washington, Moscow.

The series shows how, on both sides of the conflict, lives change over the years. The United States could guarantee rising prosperity for most of its people and pay the arms bill over five decades. The Soviet Union could not; defense expenditure crippled the economy. Pressure to change and the consequences of perestroika broke the system and brought down the USSR in the end.

A mammoth film undertaking like *Cold War* can become a logistic nightmare. Our teams dodged shells and bombs in Afghanistan, battled against freezing conditions in Russia, had their equipment stolen in Miami, and exhausted the bureaucracy in Havana. Director of photography Jim Howlett and sound recordist Peter Eason were the mainstay of a filming schedule that lasted almost three years and spanned thirty-one countries. Month after month, hours of film for cataloging arrived in London onto the desk of archivist Aileen McAllister, straight out of university. In all more than eight thousand items. Only when each clip and its source were entered into a data base was the film ready for the editing rooms. Aileen never faltered.

To make *Cold War* we needed luck. Sir Frank Roberts, the British diplomat who met Stalin in Moscow in 1941, was the first man we interviewed. A rare witness to the 1940s, he died earlier this year. George Kennan served in the U.S. embassy in Moscow in the 1930s. His famous "Long Telegram" in 1946 alerted Washington to Stalin's anti-Western activities. Kennan is, happily, still living; he gave us his first television interview in years. McGeorge Bundy, President Kennedy's aide, sought advice when we asked him to appear. He consulted Fred Friendly of CBS fame. Friendly said, "If it's for Jeremy Isaacs, do it." Bundy did and died three weeks later. Now, Friendly, too, is dead. Our series would have been the poorer if Ted Turner had waited.

And there were other sorts of luck. In Fulton, Missouri, where Churchill came to deliver his "Iron Curtain" speech, Martin Smith found, languishing in the museum, a can of 8-mm film; it had never been publicly screened. Now a film buff's amateur effort brings the scene to life, in color.

More chilling are the KGB's own home movies. Jonathan Lewis, in his film on spies, includes the KGB's record of the capture of the CIA's best agent, Dimitri Polyakov, betrayed to the KGB by Aldrich Ames. We see him caught, interrogated, tried. We don't see him shot.

Fidel Castro stalled for over a year before agreeing to an interview only weeks before we had to wrap. It is a good one. Pat Mitchell asked him twelve questions; he talked for five and a half hours. Margaret Thatcher was the only blank we drew. She is featured but was not interviewed, preferring soliloquy to joining a cast of hundreds.

I have particularly enjoyed being part of *Cold War* because these are my memories, too: the headlines on my way to school when Franklin D. Roosevelt died — between the Yalta and Potsdam agreements; the Korean

War had me wondering if I would see national service there; the Cuban missile crisis—Richard Dimbleby, on Panorama, advising a mother (I was now myself a parent) that it was safe to send her child to school. As a TV producer, I had to handle the Tonkin Gulf incident—which led to the start of the Vietnam War—on the dubious facts the Pentagon provided; in August 1968, Robert Kee and Erik Durschmied rang in to report they were on their way to Prague where Soviet tanks were rolling in. And I recall welcoming Mikhail Gorbachev to Covent Garden and daring to hope that, like that evening's opera—it was *Cinderella*—the cold war would have a happy ending. I am glad Ted Turner mixed me up with Jeremy Irons.

Cold War will be, almost immediately, accessible to everyone; all the annotated program scripts, sourcing every fact, dating every interview, identifying every frame of film and every bar of music, will very soon be on the Internet, on CNN's *Cold War* web site. This lends validity and lasting use to otherwise ephemeral reporting.

The line between journalism and history has blurred in the age of twenty-four-hour media. When I was at school, history stopped at 1900. Anything later was too recent to be serious; it was not to be trusted. But today's media record history as it happens. Our adviser John Gaddis's latest book on the cold war is called *We Now Know*; he writes with hindsight. We share that hindsight, but in the series we choose, much of the time, to conceal it, preferring to re-create the experience of not knowing how, at various crises, things were going to turn out. Timothy Garton Ash, who observed firsthand the events of 1989 in Eastern Europe, has pointed out that television cameras record, in the looks on people's faces, what they did not know at the time. Would the police they confronted in Prague, Leipzig, Berlin open fire as they did in Tiananmen Square? Television history has come of age in the last quarter-century. When I finished *The World at War* some academics doubted it had any merit. Today, in the United States, it is widely in use as a teaching tool. *Cold War* will, I hope, serve as that also. First, though, let's see how it goes on Saturday nights.

5

CNN's Cold War:
Twenty-four Hours of Moral Equivalence

Charles Krauthammer

Charles Krauthammer is a syndicated columnist. This article first appeared in the *Washington Post*, October 30, 1998. Copyright 1998, the Washington Post Co. All rights reserved.

Whoever said that history is written by the victors has not seen CNN's twenty-four-hour epic documentary *Cold War*. No, it was not written by the Soviets. But it was clearly written from the perspective of those who for years considered "cold warrior" an epithet and reviled as reactionary warmongers those, like Ronald Reagan, who insisted on victory.

Seeing the cold war presented from a vantage point that only yesterday disparaged it is an interesting experience. No doubt, you learn a lot of history in twenty-four hours (the show runs weekly through April), and you see some great new footage, including yards of hilarious socialist-realist, happy-worker propaganda.

But *Cold War*'s bias is deep and disturbing. It consists of a relentless attempt to find moral equivalence between the two sides. This is not easy, seeing as millions of Poles, Hungarians, Czechs, Germans, and others wept with joy when liberated from one side and permitted to join the other. *Cold War* tries nonetheless. Its specialty is subtly juxtaposing facts to implicate the West in Soviet nastiness. Take the Soviets' brutal 1956 invasion of Hungary: "Khrushchev had ordered the attack after the Americans had let him understand that, as far as Eisenhower was concerned, Hungary belonged in the Soviet sphere of influence."

Now, Khrushchev ordered the attack because permitting the germ of freedom anywhere in his prison-house of nations threatened the entire Soviet empire. Yet *Cold War* cleverly manages to present Eisenhower's forced acquiescence as coconspiracy. What in God's name was Eisenhower supposed to do? Start World War III?

Generally, the authors of this show are rather down on World War III. But in this instance—and in the erection of the Berlin Wall in 1961—the

American refusal to intervene and risk world war is presented as moral indifference and great power cynicism: Ike and JFK as enablers (to use a current term) of Soviet oppression.

Or consider a tiny segment on Stalin's brutal industrialization of the USSR. It features footage of Americans ("Stalin's industrial drive soon attracted American experts"), greedy and cynical ("Communist ideology didn't worry them. Unlike the Russians, they were free to go when the job was over"), frolicking by the seaside even as "Soviet muscles strained to raise dams and blast furnaces." So now we know who was behind one of the most inhuman forced industrializations in history.

In episode six ("Reds 1948–1953"), however, subtlety is abandoned. The premise is explicit: There was paranoia on both sides of the Iron Curtain. "Both sides turned their fear inward against their own people. They hunted the enemy within." In the Soviet Union it produced the Gulag; in the United States, the red scare. Half the show on one, half on the other.

This is moral equivalence with a sledgehammer. Forget the fact that the Gulag long predates the cold war and derives instead from the savage intolerance of Leninism. The Gulag—a vast continental system of arrest, torture, disappearance, execution, forced labor, starvation—is juxtaposed with what? The Hollywood Ten!

Jailed, we are told. But not told that the sentences ranged from four to ten months. For about a decade, too, they were blacklisted. Some were forced to write under pseudonyms.

The horror. Yes, of course, this shouldn't have happened. It is a blot on our history that these men's civil rights were trampled. But a blot is no mirror to an ocean of blood.

Enter the one U.S. "red scare" execution of the cold war, the Rosenbergs. (This to match the twenty million to forty million murdered by Stalin alone.) Extensive footage of the Rosenbergs' lawyer saying that the judge condemned them to death for craven political reasons. What were they convicted of? "Spying for the Soviet Union," we are told. What kind of spying? No mention. A high schooler watching this might imagine they passed a picture of a power plant to a Soviet attaché.

The companion volume does admit that they gave Stalin secrets of the atomic bomb. It then offers this explanation: "Rosenberg was at the center of a network of spies who felt uncomfortable that the United States was the sole owner of the key to atomic warfare." *Uncomfortable*. That one of most prodigious murderers in history lacked the deadliest weapon ever devised. No doubt, treason relieved the poor man's unease.

Then lots of neat footage on Alger Hiss — offered in perfect agnosticism about his guilt. But this should not surprise. After all, this and every other episode of *Cold War* ends abruptly and dramatically with the credit line, Series Concept, Ted Turner. As the conceptmeister told the *Post*: "A lot of students got killed at Tiananmen Square, but I remember several students got killed at Kent State. And, remember, they have a lot more students than we do."

6

Letter to the Editor of the *Washington Post*

Sir Jeremy Isaacs

Jeremy Isaacs was executive producer on *Cold War*. He and Taylor Downing wrote the accompanying book. This letter first appeared in the *Washington Post*, November 7, 1998.

I was interested to read Charles Krauthammer's view of the TV series *Cold War*, of which I am coexecutive producer with Pat Mitchell of CNN/ Time Productions [op-ed, October 30, 1998]. "Moral equivalence" plainly lies in the eyes of the beholder.

It is true that in *Cold War* we present a narrative to which eyewitnesses from the Soviet Union contribute. So do Hungarians, Poles, Czechoslovaks, Germans. It is untrue that we present an equivalence, moral or otherwise, between the two protagonists. Anyone watching the series will have noted George Kennan's vivid description of the vileness of Stalin and his regime; Lord Annan's comparison of Soviets and Nazis; Wolfgang Leonhard's account of Soviet takeover techniques; Czechoslovaks' description of the Kremlin's bullying of Masaryk and the communist takeover in 1948.

I am grateful to Krauthammer for urging viewers to watch the "Reds" episode. In it we contrast McCarthyism, a spasm, during which one can point to two executions, the Rosenbergs, convicted, as we state, of treason, with a system that sent millions to their deaths in the Gulag. In the next episode, Soviet tanks shoot down Hungarians in Budapest.

As the series progresses, we see the Soviets crushing the other free peoples Krauthammer cites in Prague, in Warsaw, and in Berlin. In none of these cases did the West intervene because none, as we state, justified risking the start of a third world war. Sensibly, if regretfully, the West for decades left the peoples of Eastern Europe to their fate behind the Iron

Curtain that marked post–World War II spheres of influence. They endured.

In 1989, at the end of the communist despotism that ruled their lives, *Cold War* shows their heroism and their rejoicing. The right side won. If Krauthammer keeps watching, he will get the point in the end.

7

Revolutionary Dreams

Charles Krauthammer

Charles Krauthammer is a syndicated columnist. This article first appeared in the *Washington Post*, January 1, 1999. Copyright 1999, the Washington Post Co. All rights reserved.

Jeremy Isaacs, coproducer of the CNN series *Cold War*, is unhappy with my recent critique [op-ed, October 30, 1998] of his handiwork. I charged that his twenty-four-part epic documentary is shot through with tendentious U.S.-Soviet "moral equivalence." He wrote the *Washington Post* to deny the charge ["Free for All," November 7, 1998]. "Moral equivalence," he protests, "lies in the eyes of the beholder."

Well, behold this: The episode on the Berlin Wall features a riveting eyewitness account of an East German escapee dying in the no-man's-land at the wall: "It was so heartrending that in the middle of nowhere was a human dying and two groups were facing each other, too worried to act."

Two groups, American on one side, Soviet on the other, coldly letting this young man die. This is a perfect metaphor for the series' view of the cold war: Those who erected the wall, then murdered the man as he sought freedom in the West, share culpability with the Americans who dared not rescue him for fear of sparking an incident, perhaps a war.

Then, this summary, a perfect capsule of the moral symmetry practiced in Isaacs's show: "The wall was the supreme symbol of the cold war's cruelty and Europe's division." Rubbish. The wall was the supreme symbol of Soviet cruelty in turning half a continent into a giant prison house and forcing half a century of division on a continent that longed to be whole and free and became so only as the Soviet Union expired.

In fact, *Cold War* often goes beyond mere moral equivalence to cheap anti-Americanism. Take episode eighteen, for example. "Backyard" is an unending catalog of American perfidy in Latin America. It concludes thus: "1990. Sandinista leader Daniel Ortega asks the Nicaraguan people to vote him president. . . . Violetta Chamorro, Ortega's opponent, narrowly won a surprise victory. Washington spent nearly $10 million backing her campaign."

Abrupt break. Dramatic theme music. Cut to titles. End of story.

Very clever. Why, in the very first free election held by the Sandinistas, did the people throw them out? The clear implication: Because America bought Chamorro's victory. After all, just minutes earlier, we had been advised that "the American dollar, and the failures of the armed left, crushed Latin American revolutionary dreams."

These "revolutionary dreams," however, belonged not to the Nicaraguan people but to the European and American left, who imagined—as *Cold War* portrays—the anti-Sandinista contras as Yankee stooges. In fact, they represented an authentic, indigenous peasant resistance to a communist dictatorship that had hijacked the anti-Somoza revolution. This is why the left was shocked by the victory of the contras and their allies in the election. It refuted all the fashionable nonsense said about the contras, nonsense *Cold War* repeats as if it were 1986.

The viewer is led to believe that Washington bought the election. But the Sandinistas were in complete control of government media, had total access to the national treasury for their campaign, and harassed the opposition with what one historian called "brownshirt tactics." Washington's help barely leveled the playing field.

Isaacs's revisionism extends not just to history but to his own show. He claims that in the egregious episode six ("Reds") on the red scare, "we contrast McCarthyism, a spasm . . . with a system that sent millions to their deaths in the Gulag."

Contrast? Spasm? Has he not seen his own show? It clearly presents the red scare here and the Gulag there as two sides of the same coin: cold war paranoia. It contains, for example, but one mention of children being urged to inform on the thought crimes of their own parents. Which side of the cold war does the show so indict? The United States!

This is, of course, a grotesque turning of history on its head. It was the Soviet Union that made national heroes of children who informed on their parents. Knowledgeable adults will wince at these falsities. But CNN is offering this series as a teaching tool for schools. How are young people to know?

How are they to know, for example, that, when a Soviet official says on camera that the Soviets invaded Afghanistan because they feared that Afghanistan's communist dictator would "turn to the Americans for help and they would put their own troops in," this is risible KGB disinformation — Jimmy Carter invading Afghanistan! — turned into post–cold war apologetics?

They will never know it watching this thoroughly tendentious production.

8

Viewer Discretion Advised

Jacob Heilbrunn

Jacob Heilbrunn is a senior editor at the *New Republic*. This article first appeared in the *New Republic*, November 9, 1998. Copyright UMI Company 1998. All rights reserved. Copyright *New Republic*, November 9, 1998.

One can only marvel at the ambition of CNN's twenty-four-week documentary series *Cold War*, which began on Sunday, September 27, 1998, and will continue through April. Personally conceived by Ted Turner, the series attempts a definitive recounting of the long, twilight struggle between the United States and the Soviet Union, based on miles of often breathtaking archival footage and interviews with everyone from Fidel Castro to ordinary citizens on both sides of the Iron Curtain.

Turner insisted that the CNN series be objective as well as comprehensive. Turner himself decided that a British producer be given the series. He wanted to avoid any hint of American triumphalism (Turner seemingly didn't mind that Britain was America's staunchest anti-Soviet ally). "The idea," British coproducer Jeremy Isaacs has said, was "to tell the story of the cold war not wrapped in Old Glory but from the viewpoints of both protagonists."

Yet this is precisely the show's problem. Isaacs's outstanding previous work is *The World at War* series about World War II. Obviously he never dreamed of giving equal time, weight, and credence to both the Nazi and Allied "viewpoints." Similarly, when it comes to the Soviet Union, neutrality is itself a kind of ideological position. You can view the cold war as a justifiable (if sometimes excessive) American struggle to contain, and ultimately defeat, a monstrous system that was intent on global expansion. Or you can view it, as the CNN series does, as a morally unintelligible contest between two equally dangerous superpowers, whose "fear" of each other constantly threatened to plunge a world full of innocent bystanders into nuclear holocaust.

So, while the CNN saga never denies the horrors of Soviet communism and even recounts some of them (as well as China's lunatic Cultural Revolution), it fails to make the connection between the barbarous internal nature of the Soviet system and its foreign policy. Instead, every effort is made to draw parallels between American misdeeds, at home and abroad, and Soviet ones. Neither Soviet communism itself nor any of its individual leaders is held to account for perpetuating the cold war. Rather, both Soviets and Americans are presented almost as victims of their equally irrational "fears."

CNN 's story begins with the 1919 World War I peace settlement, which "excluded Bolshevik Russia." The West sent troops to fight the Bolshevik revolution; "the intervention left Lenin and Stalin convinced that the West would seize any chance," the narrator, Irish Shakespearean actor Kenneth Branagh, says, "embrace any ally, in order to destroy communism." David Ortenberg, a bemedaled Red Army veteran, explains, "We knew we were fighting for the people. The poor people." Of course, by this time, Lenin had already instituted terror as an instrument of political control and was plotting his own war against Poland and supporting revolution in Germany. But Branagh agrees with Comrade Ortenberg: "There was widespread support" for the Reds in Russia.

CNN then blames the 1939 Hitler-Stalin pact on the West: "Stalin drew lessons from Munich. The Western democracies," he concluded, "would never stand up to Hitler." But, of course, the Soviet Union itself was hardly "standing up" to Hitler. The Soviets had secretly done business with Hitler's regime in the 1930s, even allowing the Wehrmacht to train on Soviet territory. Stalin's real motive in signing the pact was territorial gain in Poland and the Baltic states.

Once Hitler attacked Stalin, the Soviets became the "anti-Fascist" power — an ally of the West against Hitler. The alliance broke up after the war, a development that CNN attributes to mutual suspicion. While CNN shows Stalin setting up dictatorships in Eastern Europe, it explains such moves as rational strategizing. Consider the 1948 blockade of Berlin. The show claims that, at a "secret" London conference, the British and Americans plotted to carve up Germany. What choice, the episode implies, did the Soviets have but to respond? But there was no "secret" plan to divide up Berlin. Once the Western allies introduced a new currency for West Berlin, the Soviets, as Dennis L. Bark and David R. Gress observe in *A*

History of West Germany, had "an excuse to blockade Berlin," which, as an island of democracy, represented a standing affront to the Soviets.

Then there is the Korean War. Both the Americans and Soviets are presented as pursuing similar policies. "South of the divide, the Americans were in control," Branagh narrates. "North of the thirty-eighth parallel, the Russians were in control." Well, yes. But "control" meant one thing in the North and quite another in the South. Ten San Din, a Soviet adviser to North Korea, is trotted out to report that the North's Kim Il Sung was "the national hero of the Korean people." Why, then, did half of the North Korean POWs choose not to return to Kim Il Sung's realm, a fact CNN reports but doesn't analyze?

An episode called "Reds" is even worse. It opens with black-and-white pictures of a snow-covered Gulag and then shifts to a snarling J. Edgar Hoover denouncing communism. Branagh declares: "In the Soviet Union and in America, the cold war was fought by fear. The Soviet Union raised fences against the outside world. The Gulag, the secret universe of labor camps, swallowed the lives of millions. Both sides turned their fear inwards against their own people. They hunted the enemy within." Hoover equals Stalin?

As pictures of America in the 1950s flash by, Branagh fairly sneers that "the cold war made America invent new images for American virtue. . . . Was communism out to destroy all this? American propaganda said it was." In the United States, "leaders of the American Communist Party were jailed, and the persecution spread. Left-wing labor organizations were banned, radical groups indicted, demonstrations broken up."

The use of the passive voice makes terror seem pervasive, but this is hyperbole. Some Communists were convicted, under the Smith Act, for conspiracy to teach and advocate the overthrow of the U.S. government by force and violence. But the Communist Party of the United States of America was never banned—despite the fact that recently opened Soviet archives reveal that it was funded by the Soviets right up to Gorbachev's time. The AFL-CIO expelled communist-front labor groups from its own ranks. The series depicts the struggles over communism during the 1950s as a battle between hysterical right-wingers and "persecuted" leftists; there's no room in the story for anticommunist liberals such as Arthur Schlesinger Jr. or Walter Reuther.

By now, you'd think that no serious news organization would even implicitly lend credence to Alger Hiss's denials of espionage. The guilty verdict of Allen Weinstein's book *Perjury* has recently been confirmed by the release of the National Security Agency's Venona files, which show that the Soviet Union did indeed have hundreds of agents in the United States and that Hiss was one of them. But, in CNN's version, Hiss's guilt is never explicitly mentioned; he is portrayed as a hapless victim of a power-hungry politician. "Hiss," Branagh says, "firmly denied that he had betrayed his country. Richard Nixon, an ambitious young Republican, was convinced that Hiss was lying. Hiss was jailed for perjury. Nixon's name was made." Hiss "was jailed" after a trial by a jury of his peers, a constitutional nicety never observed for the multitudes accused of espionage in the Soviet Union.

CNN's coverage of the Rosenberg case is also muddled. "In 1953, two Americans, Julius and Ethel Rosenberg, were convicted of spying for the Soviet Union," Branagh tells his audience. "They were sentenced to death." CNN dwells on the cruelty of the sentence but does not point out in this episode that the Rosenbergs were, in fact, guilty or that their crime was the extraordinary one of handing over U.S. secrets that helped Stalin build nuclear weapons more rapidly. It is only fifteen episodes later in the series—that is, fifteen weeks later—that a passing reference calls them "KGB agents."

Branagh concludes that "the spirit of McCarthyism, the smearing of dissent as Communist treason, stained American democracy for decades. In the Soviet Union, all dissent was suppressed." But the Rosenbergs, Hiss, and other American Communists were not exactly "dissenters"; many of them were, quite consciously, agents of a hostile foreign power. As Senator Daniel Patrick Moynihan notes in his brilliant new book *Secrecy*: "The facts now in hand surely attest that the U.S. government's pursuit of alleged sympathizers and spies in the post–World War II period did not amount to persecution, still less delusion. Not a few in fact were spies, and, of these, most were left untroubled." Apparently, CNN's producers didn't think to put Moynihan on camera.

In "Make Love Not War," an episode written by feminist Germaine Greer, CNN trots out everyone from former Black Panther Bobby Seale to Allen Ginsberg to portray the United States in the 1960s as a racist, warmongering nation. "The cold war military buildup continued," Branagh says scornfully, but "an increasing minority were questioning the cost and effect on American life." (Apparently, that minority was able to increase despite the "smearing" of all "dissent.")

And the Soviet regime of that era? Nikita Khrushchev, according to his son Sergei, "believed that socialism had to be liberated. . . . It should be made more democratic." Which must be why he sent missiles to Cuba. Branagh reports that "Khrushchev believed the Soviet people would work even harder if they were freed from fear and poverty. But the cold war 's pressure to rearm"—an exogenous, abstract force that even the ruler of the Soviet Union was apparently powerless to resist—"kept the old priority for heavy industry alive, especially in the expanding defense sector."

After praising Khrushchev as a proto-Gorbachev, the series turns on him. Former KGB boss Vladimir Semichastny explains the 1964 Politburo putsch that got rid of Krushchev this way: "The fruit was overripe," and Soviet society would have rotted away under Khrushchev. Branagh concludes: "Few people missed Khrushchev. Many wanted a firm hand on the tiller again." Who are these "many" who wanted an even tougher dictatorship? Fortunately, the Soviet Union had a gifted replacement: Leonid Brezhnev. Georgi Arbatov, the former head of the Soviet Union's USA-Canada Institute, describes Brezhnev as "a sincere person . . . with a very strong conviction that he had to do his best to prevent war." No one is presented to dispute this tranquil view of the corrupt and incompetent man who sent Soviet troops into Afghanistan in 1979.

There is more. In a confused episode written by the left-wing British journalist Jonathan Steele, we learn that Africa was "fresh hunting grounds for cold war superpowers." We are repeatedly told that Cuba sent troops to aid Angola in 1974 without Soviet approval, as if that mattered, considering that the Soviets supplied the Cubans as they propped up their Angolan allies for the next decade and a half. The show points out that the Soviets did tell Castro to send fifteen thousand troops to help the Ethiopian regime of Mengistu Haile Mariam battle Somalia. After the victory, the show says, Mengistu "basked in glory"; the accompanying footage shows him being cheered by throngs of Ethiopians. No mention that the Cuban-Soviet intervention rescued a regime whose brutal Stalinist program of farm collectivization led to the starvation of hundreds of thousands of people. Treatment of the cold war in Latin America is a rehash of anti-American cliches, including howlers like the contention that Nicaragua's Sandinistas "narrowly" lost a free election in 1990. Actually Violeta Chamorro rolled up a 55 percent majority, while the Sandinistas' Daniel Ortega got 41 percent of the vote.

When it comes time to evaluate the cold war's conclusion, CNN can't bring itself to state the obvious: It was an American victory, a Soviet defeat, and, hence, a boon to millions of people around the world. The series seeks instead to portray the outcome as a victory over "fear," as a consequence of Ronald Reagan's willingness, in his second term, to pursue "better relations" with Mikhail Gorbachev. This is a half-truth. It was Reagan's tough first term, during which he raised tensions with his uncompromising denunciations of the Soviet system and with his deployment of Pershing missiles in Western Europe (over the protests of the peace movement), that showed the Soviets, already reeling from their economic failures and the Afghanistan quagmire, that they were up against a revitalized America. Suddenly, political space opened up in the Soviet Union for Mikhail Gorbachev's reforms, which began as an attempt to make the Soviets more competitive with the United States and ended as a rout.

The ultimate flaw in CNN's documentary, then, is that it retrospectively accords a patina of legitimacy to a Soviet system that was utterly illegitimate. And CNN's moral equivalence about the past has implications for the present. As we see daily on CNN, dictators from Iraq to China to Yugoslavia still menace their own peoples and challenge the United States. In that context, Ted Turner made this interesting remark apropos of *Cold War*: "We are often judgmental about people that are different from us. . . . And we don't even understand what their problems are. A lot of students got killed at Tiananmen Square, but I remember several students got killed at Kent State. And, remember, [the Chinese] have a lot more students than we do."

9

The Cold War On-Screen

Kenneth Auchincloss

Kenneth Auchincloss is editor at large at *Newsweek*. This article first appeared in *Newsweek*, November 9, 1998. Copyright 1998 Newsweek, Inc. All rights reserved. Reprinted by permission.

CNN's megaseries has been attacked as slanted. No, it's vivid, revealing, and mostly fair-minded.

Ted turner has done it again. Last year he pledged $1 billion to the United Nations, not America's favorite charity. Now he has plunged $12 million into an enormous, twenty-four-part television documentary on foreign affairs—a topic for which the American TV audience has always displayed a passionate lack of interest. The project was born at the Goodwill Games in St. Petersburg, Russia, back in 1994. Turner invited his production chief for breakfast and murmured two words: "cold war." With that, television armies around the world were mobilized and sent into battle, scouring several continents for footage on the half-century-long struggle between East and West. The CNN megaseries, which began five weeks ago and will not conclude till next April, might have been a sprawling bore or triumphalist rant. It isn't. It is vivid, revealing, and on the whole fair-minded.

Predictably, though, the project has attracted some critical small-arms fire. The cold war is a subject much explored by left-wing academic revisionists, eager to suggest that the West drove the Russians to their brutal behavior or acted, in its own way, almost as nastily. Arnold Beichman in the *Weekly Standard*, Jacob Heilbrunn in the *New Republic*, and Charles Krauthammer in the *Washington Post* all have charged that the series commits just that sort of sin, glossing over Soviet crimes or suggesting a moral equivalence between the two adversaries. I spotted what I thought were a few lapses but not enough to blot the whole series. The section on the "red scare" in the United States is long on jowly shots of Joe McCarthy and short on the genuine evidence of Soviet-led spying and subversion during the 1930s and 1940s. Alger Hiss comes across as a nice young man hounded by Richard Nixon and convicted only of "perjury." That's true, but one of his false statements was denying he had committed espionage for the Russians (the statute of limitations had run out on that). There's a rather ghoulish eyewitness account of the electrocution of Julius and Ethel Rosenberg that seems intended to win sympathy for the atomic spies. And the episode on revolutionary movements in Latin America is quite prorebel ("The American dollar and the failures of the armed left crushed Latin American revolutionary dreams"). The dreams of Allende in Chile, Castro in Cuba, and the Sandinistas in Nicaragua were mostly nightmares for their people.

But it would take a thoroughly obtuse viewer to come away from this series not thinking that the right side had won. The horror of Stalin's regime is amply documented; there's a wonderful account of a dinner party at which a waiter spills some blood-red sauce on Stalin's jacket and all the guests freeze, in the apparent belief that the man will be taken out and shot (he wasn't). The privation of life behind the Iron Curtain—empty food shelves, thwarted artistic expression, unrelenting bleakness of life—comes through in scene after scene (even the propaganda footage of smiling workers merrily exceeding their norms). Sir Jeremy Isaacs, the British coproducer (with Pat Mitchell, president of Time Inc. Television/CNN Productions), uses the same documentary techniques he brought to his excellent previous series, *The World at War*. Film clips, surprisingly fresh for a field that has been so extensively mined, are interspersed with reflections by people who played a part in the drama on both sides (there's a welcome lack of latter-day commentators). Many well-placed Russians offer now-it-can-be-told accounts of events, such as the downing of the Korean airliner in 1983, on which a candid Russian perspective has not been readily available up to now. Some of these remarks are undoubtedly self-serving, a point the critics fastened on, but the viewer should have no problem noticing when they are. And the little man gets his due; a Greek peasant praising the feisty Missouri mule he got through the Marshall Plan is a good deal more eloquent than the slightly too-frequent interjections of Fidel Castro. The most poignant figure in the series is Mikhail Gorbachev. Modern, intelligent, flexible, he introduces perestroika (restructuring) and glasnost (openness) to a society where they had been utterly alien for more than half a century. He thinks a little tinkering will streamline the socialist system; instead, his tinkerings lead to the system's collapse. He thinks a little freedom for the satellites will win Moscow their gratitude; instead, they reject communism and hasten to join the West. He wanted to end the cold war in order to strengthen the Soviet state; instead, the cold war ended with the demise of the Soviet state.

In the final episodes, Gorbachev comes close to being the hero of the drama. His role was clearly a central one at the end. But at the risk of sounding a nationalist note that is so alien to Turner's CNN, I would suggest that the real heroes were American. From Harry Truman and the Marshall Plan, to John Kennedy and the Cuban missile crisis, to Richard Nixon and détente, to Ronald Reagan and his arms control diplomacy, they managed a half century of great danger with a rare combination of adroitness and resolve. They were new to the business of world leadership. They had to conduct diplomacy in the glare of legislative oversight and public opinion. But as defense strategist Paul Nitze, who was a key American player for most of those fifty years, puts it: "We did it pretty goddam well." Yes, they did.

10

How Anti-Americanism Won the Cold War

Joseph Shattan

Joseph Shattan, a Bradley Fellow at the Heritage Foundation, is writing a book tentatively titled *Heroes of the Cold War*. This article first appeared in the *American Spectator*, January 1999.

Although Jimmy Carter has praised Ted Turner's "deep and long-standing commitment to easing the tension and disharmony between the two superpowers, world peace, nuclear arms control, environmental quality, and global sharing of news," that is not why I am certain that *Cold War*, Ted Turner's twenty-four-part, $12-million CNN documentary is an awful waste of time. Rather, I arrived at this judgment after reading the companion volume to the TV series, also called *Cold War*. Coauthored by Jeremy Isaacs (the British executive producer of the series) and Taylor Downing (another British filmmaker), and based on the scripts for the documentary, it is one of the shoddiest, most intellectually dishonest books I have ever come across.

The book's thesis is that the cold war was almost entirely America's fault. To make their case, Isaacs and Downing ignore a vast body of evidence and distort the rest. Consider their account of the cold war's origins. The authors maintain that the principal goal of Stalin's foreign policy after World War II was to establish a buffer zone along the Soviet Union's western borders, so as to ensure that his country would never be invaded from Europe again. President Roosevelt appreciated Stalin's legitimate security needs, but his successor, Harry Truman, "was largely ignorant of foreign affairs. . . . Truman's tendency was to see things in clearly defined, black-and-white terms. He lacked the patience to weigh up subtleties of argument." Unable to recognize that the Soviet Union, having suffered horrendously in World War II, was morally entitled to a sphere of influence in Eastern Europe, Truman mulishly insisted that the Russians follow through on their Yalta pledge to hold free elections in the nations they had occupied. In the face of Truman's high-handedness, "the

Soviets now understood that the era of wartime collaboration was over" and that the cold war had begun.

But if Truman, following FDR's lead, had adopted a kinder, gentler approach to Stalin, might the cold war have been averted? In his 1997 book *We Now Know*, John Lewis Gaddis, widely considered the dean of American cold war historians, argues that it would not. He cites an interview given by the former Soviet foreign minister Maxim Litvinov to CBS correspondent Richard C. Hottelet early in 1946, in which Litvinov attributed Soviet-American tensions to "the ideological conception prevailing here that the conflict between the Communist and capitalist worlds is inevitable." When Hottelet asked him what would happen if the West should suddenly grant all of Stalin's demands, Litvinov replied that "it would lead to the West's being faced, after a more or less short time, with the next series of demands." In other words, even if Truman had adopted a more conciliatory policy, it wouldn't have made the slightest difference, since the cold war was Stalin's doing, not his.

Unfortunately, despite claiming to have "benefited enormously" from Professor Gaddis's advice, neither the Litvinov interview nor any of the other evidence adduced by Gaddis to demonstrate Stalin's culpability is cited by Isaacs and Downing. If they were serious historians, such omissions would be inexplicable. But Isaacs and Downing are prosecutors, not scholars, and their objective isn't to establish the truth but to build up a case against the United States.

A particularly telling example of the authors' cavalier approach is their treatment (or, rather, nontreatment) of the Baruch Plan—the Truman administration's 1946 initiative, rejected by Moscow, to bring atomic power under international control. Some scholars have praised the Baruch Plan for its unprecedented generosity; others maintain that it didn't go far enough in meeting Stalin's legitimate concerns. But whatever their views about the plan, all those who have written about the cold war recognize that it was a historic initiative—all, that is, but Isaacs and Downing, who never quite get around to mentioning it. What they do mention is that General Curtis LeMay, who headed up America's Strategic Air Command, once admitted that if the United States had lost World War II, the Japanese would have tried him as a war criminal for his raids against their cities. They also point out that LeMay's successor, General Thomas Power, was such a hard-liner that even LeMay questioned his mental stability. Once again, facts that show the United States to have been at least reasonably conciliatory are ignored; facts suggesting that American officials were a bunch of psychos and war criminals are highlighted.

Even when the facts belie their assertions, Isaacs and Downing still charge foolishly ahead. In discussing America's decision to build a hydrogen bomb, for example, the authors describe a debate that took place between two groups of scientists. One group, led by Robert Oppenheimer, argued that for the United States to build a "superbomb" would be immoral since it would inevitably ignite a thermonuclear arms race that would endanger all of mankind; the other group, led by Edward Teller, argued that for the United States not to build a superbomb would be immoral since it would ultimately place the American people at the mercy of the Soviets. When the issue came before President Truman, he quickly decided in favor of Teller. "That night," write Isaacs and Downing, "Truman announced to the world that he was directing that a new 'so-called hydrogen or superbomb' be developed. With this announcement, he fired the starter's pistol for the ultimate arms race." As with the origins of the cold war, so with the thermonuclear arms race: The Soviets merely reacted to ill-considered American initiatives.

In his *Memoirs*, however, the actual architect of the Soviet hydrogen bomb, Andrei Sakharov, offered a strikingly different account of the bomb's origins:

> The dispute over [Teller's and Oppenheimer's] opposing stands continues to this day, but the facts that have come to light about the state of affairs in the late 1940's support Teller's point of view. The Soviet government (or, more properly, those in power: Stalin, Beria, and company) already understood the potential of the new weapon, and nothing would have dissuaded them from going forward with its development. Any U.S. move toward abandoning or suspending work on a thermonuclear weapon would have been perceived either as a cunning, deceitful maneuver or as evidence of stupidity or weakness. In any case, the Soviet reaction would have been the same: to avoid a possible trap, and to exploit the adversary's folly at the earliest opportunity.

Far from "firing the starter's pistol for the ultimate arms race," then, Truman's 1950 decision to proceed with the development of an H-bomb simply meant that Washington had finally decided to embark on a course of action to which Moscow was already committed. Isaacs and Downing claim to have based their narrative on "the latest available knowledge on a range of cold war issues," yet Sakharov's autobiography, published in 1990, appears to have escaped their notice.

If Isaacs and Downing go to extreme lengths to convict Washington of original sin, they are equally assiduous in their efforts to absolve Moscow of all wrongdoing. Consider their treatment of the Berlin Wall. Though it is generally thought of as the structure that best epitomizes the repressive essence of totalitarianism—a word, incidentally, that never appears in *Cold War*, which prefers to characterize communist regimes as "authoritarian" or, at worst, "rigidly authoritarian"—for Isaacs and Downing the wall is a testament to Khrushchev's essential moderation. As they see it, the constant stream of Germans from East to West Berlin threatened the stability of the East German state. To stanch the human hemorrhage, Khrushchev could do one of two things: either expel the Americans, British, and French from West Berlin or build a fence of some sort to block the exodus. But any attempt to eject the Western powers from Berlin carried the risk of nuclear war. Although "no one in the Kremlin liked the idea of fencing off West Berlin; it reflected badly on the Communist way of life," Khrushchev decided to erect the wall because "building it was a way of avoiding direct military conflict." Viewed in this light, the Berlin Wall emerges as a triumph of creative Soviet statesmanship, a daring effort to save the world from nuclear catastrophe.

Isaacs and Downing offer a similarly pro-Soviet reading of the Cuban missile crisis. Although most cold war historians believe that a principal motive behind the Kremlin's decision to place nuclear-armed missiles in Cuba was to force a renegotiation of the Berlin issue on terms more favorable to Moscow, Isaacs and Downing fail even to consider this possibility. Instead, they argue that Khrushchev's action was a perfectly understandable response to an intolerable provocation:

> By 1962 a million U.S. soldiers were stationed in more than two hundred
> foreign bases, all threatening the Soviet Union, from Greenland to Tur-

key, from Portugal to the Philippines. There were listening posts and USAF facilities in Iran and Pakistan, and an electronic monitoring station in Ethiopia. Three and a half million troops belonging to America's allies were garrisoned around the Soviet Union's borders. There were American nuclear warheads in Italy, the United Kingdom and Turkey. Khrushchev felt surrounded.

Placing missiles in Cuba was the Soviet David's morally justified attempt to give the American Goliath a taste of his own medicine.

Sometimes the authors simply ignore blatant examples of Soviet aggressiveness. During the 1956 Suez Crisis—what Isaacs and Downing call "the Anglo-French-Israeli aggression against Egypt"—Soviet prime minister Bulganin sent notes to Britain, France, and Israel threatening them with rocket attacks. "In what situation would Britain find herself," Bulganin asked Britain's Anthony Eden, "if she were attacked by stronger states, possessing all types of modern destructive weapons? And such countries could, at the present time, refrain from sending naval or air forces to the shores of Britain and use other means—for instance, rocket weapons." As Henry Kissinger has observed, this was "the first explicit Soviet threat of rocket attacks against a Western ally"—yet it goes entirely unmentioned in *Cold War*. (By contrast, Eisenhower is accused of attempting "to bully the Communists into a negotiated peace" in Korea by threatening to use nuclear weapons against China in 1953.)

But it is in their attempted whitewash of Soviet aggression in Afghanistan that Isaacs and Downing truly outdo themselves. The Soviet invasion of Afghanistan, they argue, was undertaken purely for defensive reasons. "The Kremlin was alarmed by the militant Islamic regimes of Southwest Asia and feared that [Afghan dictator Hafizullah] Amin would make an alliance with Pakistan and then with China." But Kremlin leaders quickly realized that the war was unwinnable and began casting about for a face-saving way out:

> From the archives in Moscow, we now know that the Soviets were trying to disengage honorably, leaving behind a friendly regime in Kabul. However, the talks were premature. Pakistan did not want peace; like the United States it preferred to see the Soviets tied down in Afghanistan.

The United States never had any real expectation that Moscow would withdraw. It concentrated instead on supplying arms to the Mujahedeen and in letting the Soviet Union "bleed." Talks dragged on for year after year, but got nowhere. . . . The United States, committed to winning the Cold War, was not about to let the Soviets off the hook. The bloodletting continued.

In short, Washington, not Moscow, was responsible for prolonging the carnage in Afghanistan.

Which brings us to Ronald Wilson Reagan, the American president most committed to winning the cold war and the villain of *Cold War*. Isaacs and Downing find him entirely devoid of redeeming characteristics. "Reagan's world was like an old Hollywood movie; he saw things in simple terms of right and wrong, with the Communists as the bad guys and the West leading a 'crusade for freedom.' . . . Any conflict, anywhere in the world, was liable to be overlaid with this simplistic vision of an ideological crusade against communism."

But Reagan was worse than a simpleton; he was a friend of tyrants everywhere:

Right-wing military juntas, despite their despicable treatment of opponents, received U.S. support. President Zia of Pakistan made it clear that, even with U.S. aid, he still wanted to develop his own nuclear weapons. Before the Falklands War between Britain and Argentina in 1982, the United States supported the Argentine generals, with their cruel record on human rights, because of their anti-Communist stance, as well as the support they gave the Contras. In El Salvador, Guatemala and Honduras, covert U.S. aid helped arm the death squads that terrorized the countryside. America's share in the international arms trade increased during the Reagan years. All this came as a consequence of Reagan's "noble cause" of fighting communism.

Needless to say, the democratization of Latin America that occurred during Reagan's presidency goes unremarked in *Cold War*.

As if such villainy weren't enough, Reagan compounded his sins by "accusing Moscow of lying, cheating, and using any means to achieve the objective of 'world revolution'; the Kremlin merely noted that the new team in Washington lacked 'political tact and courtesy.'" (Actually, Moscow went a good deal further than that, regularly comparing Reagan to Hitler and equating the United States with Nazi Germany.) Poor Kremlinites! In the face of Reagan's relentless propaganda barrage, they "had no alternative policy but to reiterate a belief in détente and strategic arms control." But the fiercely anticommunist Reagan didn't give a fig for détente, and his determination to achieve "the militarization of outer space" through SDI threatened arms control. All this came as a terrible blow to the Kremlin and especially to its leader, Yuri Andropov. "Andropov, unwell and confined to a kidney-dialysis machine at a clinic outside Moscow, saw all his hopes for peaceful co-existence shattered."

Fortunately, Andropov's protégé, Mikhail Gorbachev, picked up his fallen sponsor's banner and eventually brought the cold war to a peaceful end. Exactly why he did so is unclear to Isaacs and Downing, but on one point they are adamant: It had nothing to do with Ronald Reagan's policies:

> Reagan remained convinced that U.S. strength and determination had caused the Soviets to give in and had forced them to the negotiating table. What he never fully recognized in Gorbachev, despite the warm rapport that grew up between the two men, was that here was a Soviet leader with a new line of thinking who no longer fitted the mold of the past. Gorbachev, in countless speeches, stressed his commitment to arms reduction and his unwillingness to play the games of his predecessors; confrontation was simply not a stable basis for peace, he argued. Compromise, mutual trust, and co-operation would be the way forward. . . . A stop had to be called, and Gorbachev called it.

So now we know. Although Harry Truman started the cold war, and Ronald Reagan exacerbated it, it was Mikhail Gorbachev, the reforming Soviet idealist, who finally ended it. And he did so, apparently, out of the sheer goodness of his heart. To suggest otherwise is to leave open the possibility that American statecraft had something to do with the Soviet turnabout, yet the whole point of *Cold War* is to demonstrate the futility, fatuousness, and utter foolishness of U.S. foreign policy.

The only genuinely interesting question posed by this wretched book is why serious historians like Gaddis, Lawrence Freedman, and Vladislav

Zubock—all cited in the book's preface—allowed themselves to be associated with it. My guess is that billionaire Ted offered them a consultant's fee too generous to refuse—but perhaps I'm overly cynical. Whatever the reason, it is abundantly clear that anti-Americanism, not a desire to get at the truth of things, is the animating passion behind *Cold War*.

11

The View from Inside:
Answering Some Criticism

John Lewis Gaddis

John Lewis Gaddis is the Robert A. Lovett Professor of History at Yale University. He is
the author, most recently, of We Now Know: Rethinking Cold War History and served as a
historical consultant for CNN's Cold War. This article first appeared in the New York Times,
January 9, 1999. Copyright 1999, John Lewis Gaddis.

It has always been hard to view the cold war dispassionately, so it's no
surprise that CNN's televised version has provoked controversy. Ted Turner's involvement alone—he conceived the series—would have insured
that. Then there's the fact that historians are still hotly debating the significance of new evidence from the former Soviet Union, Eastern Europe,
and China. And of course visual images always pack more of an emotional
punch than the printed page, especially the academic prose in which most
cold war history has been written.

When I signed on as a consultant to *Cold War*, therefore, I knew that
it was going to be a great white whale and that harpoons would fly from
several directions. It's been interesting over the last four months, though,
to see their trajectories.

First, there has been the charge that it isn't scholarly. True enough in
a traditional sense. Video archives are still unfamiliar to most historians;
nor can one pitch a television presentation at the level one might for, say,
an annual meeting of the American Historical Association. But surely
visual evidence is no less valid a guide to the past than what is put down
on paper. The real problem is that previous television histories haven't
always been careful in citing their sources.

Cold War breaks new ground in this regard. Every scrap of film used
has been authenticated and documented; full versions of its five-hundred-
plus interviews are to be made available on-line, and there was careful
coordination throughout with the Cold War International History Project
and the National Security Archive, the principal centers for assessing

recently released documents on cold war history. The interviews are to be on the archive's web site: www.seas.gwu.edu/nsarchive/.

Second, some critics say too much is left out. *Cold War* has twenty-four episodes of forty-six minutes each, not counting the commercials that helped pay the bills. This makes it the longest television documentary since its coproducer, Sir Jeremy Isaacs, completed his classic series on World War II, *World at War*, a quarter-century ago. But the cold war lasted four and a half decades, not seven years, so even this much airtime left a lot that we couldn't cover. The critics, particularly the historians, have noticed: One early review listing all that we had neglected in a single episode was about twice as long as its actual script.

Triage, though, comes with the territory. A clear narrative is as vital in doing history as compelling dramatization is in theater: Both involve selecting what is really important and leaving the rest aside. How that is done, then, becomes critical.

Third, other critics say *Cold War* tells the story from a particular point of view. Correct, but I would argue that our selection criteria were methodological, not ideological. Mr. Turner insisted that the series reflect an international perspective, hence its global coverage and its reliance on consultants from Russia and Britain as well as the United States. Mr. Isaacs, in turn, determined the format: minimal narration, interviews only with participants in the events (not talking-head historians), and a particular focus on the cold war's impact on ordinary people's lives.

As a consequence, the tone is neither as celebratory nor as condemnatory as some of our critics would have liked. We did not try to settle old arguments about responsibility for the cold war. Instead we tried to allow all kinds of people simply to tell their stories: most surviving leaders, to be sure, but also a Berlin baby-sitter, a Russian rocket scientist, a Hungarian street fighter, a Cuban farmer, an Afghan mullah, an American housewife.

Finally, we've heard the complaint that the series suggests moral equivalency. Our playing down of ideology has upset the neoconservative right, which seems to harbor deep fears that Mr. Turner has been hoping all along to transform the cold war into the "goodwill games"—that he wants a history devoid of moral distinctions.

The tapes speak for themselves on this issue. Because I use them in my classes, I've watched the responses of several hundred Yale undergraduates to certain events portrayed: the Red Army rapes in Germany in 1945, the crushing of the Hungarian uprising in 1956, the suppression of Prague Spring in 1968, the invasion of Afghanistan in 1979, and the persecution of dissidents in the Soviet Union and Eastern Europe throughout the cold war. I see few if any students who come away convinced that the two sides in this struggle were morally equivalent. Most would find the notion laughable.

What they do come away with is an awareness of moral ambiguity, which is quite a different thing. The cold war was full of instances in which moral priorities competed with one another. Was it right, for example, for the CIA to subvert the 1948 Italian elections to prevent the kind of communist takeover that had occurred that year in Czechoslovakia? How, within the United States, did one balance the requirements of internal security against those of civil liberties? Could one justify reliance on nuclear weapons to deter aggression when the consequences of using them would have been far worse? Should the West have risked war to prevent the erection of the Berlin Wall? Did Washington's fears that it might "lose" the cold war in the Third World excuse all it did there? These are tough questions, but it is hardly moral equivalency to raise them. It was, indeed, precisely the inability of the "other side" to confront similar issues that ultimately eroded whatever legitimacy it had left in the cold war. Taking morality seriously means posing unsettling dilemmas, not providing smug and self-congratulatory answers.

12

Finding a Moral Difference between the United States and the Soviets

Ronald Radosh

Ronald Radosh is the coauthor of, among other books, *The Rosenberg File: A Search for the Truth* and *The Amerasia Spy Case: Prelude to McCarthyism*. This article first appeared in the *New York Times*, January 9, 1999. Copyright 1999, Ronald Radosh.

Ted Turner and the producers Jeremy Isaacs and Pat Mitchell have managed to produce an often riveting and generally comprehensive account of the cold war that will probably become the source most used to acquaint young generations with its history.

Anyone who doubts that there was a fundamental struggle between the forces of democracy based in the West, with its thriving civil society, and those of the totalitarian camp, led by Stalin and his successors, will find stark and powerful evidence of what it meant to try to lead a normal life in the so-called socialist camp. Watching clips of the Soviet invasion of Hungary in 1956 and the suppression of Prague Spring in 1968, one can't help being moved by the courage and commitment of the first generation of Soviet bloc dissidents. As one of them says, the Soviets had to suppress them; they were afraid of their "becoming an organized political force." It was, another says, a system that "produced only evil."

The final episode gives the last word to President Vaclav Havel of the Czech Republic, who says that communism simply was an affront to the normal desires of human beings just moments after we see Fidel Castro reaffirming his commitment to the communist ideology. The moral difference is starkly presented for those who think the long conflict was simply an unnecessary fight between two imperial superpowers vying for hegemony.

It is more unforgivable then that this message has been undermined by some abhorrent episodes, which suggest a moral equivalence between the Soviet bloc and the democratic Western allies. To me, the single worst episode was "Reds" (the sixth program), because it compares the epoch of

Stalinism and the Gulag to that of McCarthyism in the United States. In both countries, the narrator, Kenneth Branagh, states: "The cold war was fought by fear. . . . Both sides turned their fear inwards against their own people. They hunted the enemy within." The millions killed by Stalin are somehow to be equated with the few who were blacklisted or lost teaching jobs.

The ideological bias in these episodes is usually implied by combining selected facts in a one-sided way. Although the most recent evidence has proved that Alger Hiss was a Soviet spy for decades, for instance, he is presented as a noble figure hounded by an evil Richard Nixon. "Hiss," we are told, "firmly denied that he had betrayed his country. Richard Nixon, an ambitious young Republican, was convinced that Hiss was lying. Hiss was jailed for perjury. Nixon's name was made." The documentary does not say that Hiss was guilty, suggesting that Nixon unfairly did him in.

As for Julius Rosenberg, who the latest evidence shows was a Soviet agent who put together a network of spies, viewers are left with the impression—after hearing the grisly details of the execution—that, just as Stalin killed his dissenters, America killed its own. "The spirit of McCarthyism, the smearing of dissent as Communist treason," Mr. Branagh says, "stained American democracy for decades. In the Soviet Union, all dissent was suppressed." But Hiss and Rosenberg were not arrested and found guilty for dissent. They were Soviet agents. There is also an overly sympathetic slant when it comes to Central America and the Caribbean. Unlike the last episode, these episodes present the United States as the oppressor, while Fidel Castro is presented as a hero and given a disproportionate amount of airtime. He is never challenged in any of his arguments. The series says that Castro turned to the Soviets only after the Bay of Pigs invasion in 1961. New evidence showing that Castro made military agreements with the Soviets before the Bay of Pigs and had privately made clear his Marxist allegiance, already available before the series was finished, is simply ignored.

The series also suggests that Daniel Ortega Saavedra and the Sandinista revolutionaries freed Nicaragua in 1979 from an American-backed dictator and that, when their power collapsed, it was because of fierce American opposition. In "Backyard," we hear that in 1990 "Ortega asks the Nicaraguan people to vote him President. . . . Violeta Chamorro,

Ortega's opponent, narrowly won a surprise victory. Washington spent nearly $10 million backing her campaign."

The implication is that, were it not for the overwhelming political and monetary intervention of the United States, the revolution would have stayed in power. But those who were there to monitor the election, as this writer was, saw that the Sandinistas had a virtual monopoly on government-provided campaign funds and resources and that it regularly interfered with opposition freedom during the campaign. The opposition, the historian Robert Kagan notes, "spent a little more than half of what the Sandinistas spent." Despite this, Chamorro obtained a 55 percent majority, while Ortega received only 41 percent of the vote. The filmmakers focused on the voices of ordinary people who lived in the cold war era. But whose voices did they choose? We get to hear the blacklisted writer Ring Lardner Jr., a committed member of the American Communist Party, rather than, say, Edward Dmytryk, a director and one of the Hollywood Ten who broke with communism. We see the screenwriter John Howard Lawson yelling at members of the House Committee on Un-American Activities, but we do not hear from his son, Jeff Lawson, who has written in his new book that his father "believed that Russia was a paradise and could do no wrong" and that he turned "a blind eye to Soviet reality." There are scores of people who criticized communism but vigorously supported the civil liberties of its supporters, but we don't hear from them. Had such a witness appeared, the presentation might indeed have provided some real balance.

Throughout, leftists are presented as heroes unfairly persecuted. We see mobs attack Paul Robeson at the famous Peeksill, New York, concert in the late 1940s; we are not told that Robeson was a lifelong acolyte of the Stalin regime and opposed civil liberties for those on the left with whom he disagreed.

Some critics have praised the series for not having the proverbial "talking heads" so familiar from other documentaries. In my view, this is a weakness. Knowledgeable commentators could have put events in context, corrected some of the absurdities offered by self-interested contemporaries, and separated truth from falsehood. No amount of powerful film and remembrances by observers can compensate for the absence of informed commentary.

13

Revisiting the Cold War

Raymond A. Schroth

Jesuit father Raymond A. Schroth is assistant dean of Fordham College, Rose Hill. This article first appeared in the *National Catholic Reporter*, January 29, 1999. Copyright National Catholic Reporter Publishing Company, 1999. All rights reserved.

When we arrived in Mannheim, Germany, in January 1956 as brand-new second lieutenants in the Sixty-seventh Antiaircraft Artillery Battalion (automated weapons, self-propelled) to "play our part on the NATO team," our commanding officer, Lieutenant Colonel Gershon, took us aside for some motivational words. His analysis of a number of crucial factors—the weather, the condition of the harvest, and so on—made it highly probable that this was the season Russia was going to attack.

My job when the alert sounded was to lead the four tanks (really a tank body with a revolving twin 40-mm gun in its turret) and four half-tracks armed with 50-caliber machine guns out the gate and down to a bridge over the Rhine River and save that bridge from the Russians—either shoot them down if they flew in low or mow them down if they attacked on land. But after a while we didn't have to be strategic geniuses to realize that our part on this "team" was basically symbolic. We were a tripwire, holding the enemy for whatever time it took for the big missiles with the nuclear warheads to float through the stratosphere and reduce both us and them to radioactive dust.

For anyone old enough to remember President Franklin Roosevelt's return from Yalta and who, as either an observer or participant, has lived through the events portrayed in CNN's controversial twenty-four-part documentary on the history of the cold war, the weekly series is a chance to relive some of the best and worst moments of our time.

For all those born later, for whom the Cuban missile crisis is but a page in the history book and the Vietnam War a psychological or moral burden that his or her Vietnam veteran father carries silently through the day until it awakens him at night, the series is a unique chance for today's college generation to enter the life histories of its parents and grandparents. Some episodes drag. Others should chill the bones of anyone who allows the images and words to have their effect. A Russian veteran of the Afghanistan invasion says: "We rounded up women and children, poured kerosene on them and set them on fire. It was cruel. We did it. But we had to. They had been torturing our wounded soldiers with knives." And: "A young soldier might kill just to test his gun, or to see what the insides of a human being look like. . . . It's like being drunk on blood." A CIA operative who directed our gun shipments to the Afghanistan Islamic radicals, who were anticommunist, says, without blinking an eye, "It was our goals and their blood."

Five years ago, Ted Turner, perhaps moved by the same spirit that led him to establish the Good Will Games when the Americans boycotted the Moscow Olympics to protest Russia's Afghanistan invasion, reached out to Sir Jeremy Isaacs to do a documentary on the cold war with a sense of urgency, before the participants were dead. Isaacs had produced the great TV documentary on World War II, *The World at War*, narrated by Laurence Olivier.

But what point of view would inform the documentary? A creator can achieve his purpose with a variety of editorial decisions: careful editing of file footage, selecting the participants to be interviewed, voice-over narration, scholarly "talking heads" who explain the significance of what we have just seen. The Turner-Isaacs team determined that this story would (1) be evenhanded, rather than the story of a victory from the "victors'" point of view; (2) although Olivier protégé Kenneth Branagh would narrate a script by about a half-dozen writers, they would tell the story from the bottom up, through participants—famous and unknown—on both sides. No talking heads to explain what the pictures meant. When the main characters are still alive—or even, like Clark Clifford, at the brink of death, or old but still quick, like George F. Kennan—we hear directly from them. So, too, we hear from all the living ex-presidents, except Reagan. We hear from Robert McNamara, who sees more rational genius than insanity in the strategy of mutual assured destruction (MAD); Soviet ambassador Anatoly Dobrynin; North Vietnamese military mastermind General Vo Nguyen Giap; and Czech president-playwright Vaclav Havel.

And, inevitably, there is Henry Kissinger—who, among other things, engineered several of the least moral strategies the United States employed, including the overthrow of the democratically elected Salvador Allende government in Chile and the U.S. carpet bombing of Hanoi. Bombs fell not so much to force Hanoi to the conference table, as the script says, but to mollify South Vietnam's Premier Thieu, who feared—correctly—that the United States would abandon him.

But we are moved less by the great men than by the scores—sometimes millions—of men and women we never heard of before but who endured the cold war's hardships or witnessed its slaughters.

During the Berlin airlift, a hungry and grateful teenager cheers on an American pilot by telling the pilot he cares more for his freedom than for food. As the East Germans wall off East from West Berlin, the camera lingers on an East German border guard. Suddenly he turns, runs toward the camera, and leaps over the barbed wire separating him from the West.

When Soviet tanks roll into Lithuania, one nearly crushes a young woman protester under its treads. Isaacs's researchers found both the guard and the girl for interviews.

In the opening episode, when U.S. troops first meet the Russian army face-to-face at the Elbe River in the last days of the war in Europe, an American GI, who has never seen a Russian before, discovers that they look like anyone else: "They could have been Americans."

If CNN had interviewed *this* cold war vet, I would have recalled freezing nights on maneuvers along the Czech border in 1956, as we listened to the news during the Hungarian uprising. With our tanks and half-tracks, we thought, we had just the weapons to save the "freedom fighters" from the Russians. Maybe we would be going in. American political conservatives do not like this series. Jacob Heilbrun in the *New Republic* (November 9, 1998), syndicated columnist Charles Krautham- mer in the *New York Daily News* (November 2, 1998, and January 4), and Ronald Radosh in the *New York Times* (January 9) blast what they consider its "moral equivalence" approach, as if the cold war had not been a struggle between good and evil but between two world powers somehow equally responsible for its crimes.

Criticisms focus on the episode "Reds," where, Branagh says, "Both sides turned their fear inwards against their own people. They hunted the enemy within." In America, this fear expressed itself in McCarthyism; in Russia, the Gulag.

The script says Alger Hiss was convicted of perjury without adding that the most recent scholarship says he was a spy. For me, the two stories fit awkwardly in the same hour. But in no way does CNN imply that America's pursuit of internal communism was morally equal to Stalin's sending six million suspected dissenters to prison camps.

Indeed it is hard for me to see how anyone who actually watched the whole twenty-four hours could conclude anything but that Stalin and, to varying degrees, most of his successors were ruthless, sometimes blood-thirsty monsters. And that communism as a system failed not because we outgunned it but because it was rotten at the core because it had a false understanding of human nature. It did not see what the boy in Berlin saw, that freedom was worth more than bread.

Longer than this little debate, I hope we will remember the images. Above all the jubilant faces on the crowds of East Berliners who poured through the gate and destroyed the wall when Mikhail Gorbachev—if anyone, the true hero of this sorry time—decided the Soviet Union would not use force to stop the Russian satellites yearning to breathe free.

And I hope we remember the corpses: two million killed by our bombings of North Korea; those machine-gunned on the steps of the cathedral in San Salvador; Archbishop Oscar Romero in his coffin; nuns raped, killed, and buried by Salvadoran military; seventy naked Romanians executed and displayed.

Today, if the cold war is "dead," we can still wonder about what will take its place in defining America's national purpose.

"Deterrence kept the peace," says CNN, "by keeping us in a perma-nent state of alarm." Against whom will we arm ourselves, if that's what it takes to maintain our military-industrial "way of life"? Internally, against Central American immigrants and welfare mothers? Internationally, Fidel Castro, Arab terrorists we initially armed in Afghanistan, and Saddam Hussein have replaced Stalin and Mao Tse-tung. Our government is proud that we may have killed sixteen hundred Republican Guards in the recent bombings.

We have killed so many people—"for good reasons"—that a corpse, unless he or she represents someone's vested interest, is no longer a human being, at most a statistic and an anonymous picture in a documentary.

At the end of the twenty-four hours of *Cold War*, one question persists: Will we ever have a leader who can inspire us by our hopes rather than our fears?

14

Persecution Mania

Mark Steyn

Mark Steyn is a columnist for Britain's *Daily Telegraph* and Canada's *National Post*. This article first appeared in the London *Spectator*, March 6, 1999. Copyright 1999, Mark Steyn.

Are you now or have you ever been a member of the Communist Party?" What's so wrong with asking that question? And what's so wrong with answering it? Elia Kazan did: He had once been a member of the Communist Party, and he named a few others who had been as well—some with their consent, though others felt and continue to feel betrayed. Kazan was not furtive or shameful about what he did. After testifying to Congress in 1952, he took out a full-page ad in the *New York Times* calling communism a "dangerous and alien conspiracy" and urging American liberals to "speak out" against it.

Half a century later, we're still waiting. But, on Oscar night later this month, American liberals will speak out—against Elia Kazan. Blacklisted authors, the Committee Against Silence, the National Alliance Against Racist and Political Repression, the Los Angeles and Orange County Green Parties, the California Association of Professional Scientists, and many other groups will protest at the "lifetime achievement" award being given to the director. In the movie business the cold war remains the last good war, the only one in which Hollywood itself took the heavy blows. A year or two back, I was out in Los Angeles taking part in some debate about movies and, apropos the cinematic depiction of persecution, I scoffed, "When was the last time anyone in Hollywood was persecuted?" "The 1950s," snapped Lynda Obst, the producer of *Sleepless in Seattle*. I didn't quite know how to explain to Lynda that what happened in America in the fifties was not what most societies have traditionally understood by "persecution": For example, Bernard Gordon, a McCarthy-persecuted writer who's organizing the protest against Kazan, was obliged to work under assumed names and only recently received his proper screen credit for *Day of the Trids* and *Hellcats of the Navy*. I think my old Vermont neighbor Alexander Solzhenitsyn would have regarded being forced to adopt a nom de plume as strictly Persecution Lite. But who knows? To deny a person the right to celebrity is arguably the most American form of oppression you could devise. Perhaps that's why the fact that the Soviet Union went belly up a decade ago seems barely to have impinged on showbiz proponents of the theory of "moral equivalence."

Then there is the TV series *Cold War*, the Jeremy Isaacs behemoth currently lumbering along on CNN. "The idea," Sir Jeremy explained, with disarming honesty, "was to tell the story of the cold war not wrapped in Old Glory but from the viewpoints of both protagonists"—not a courtesy he extended, on his previous epic, *The World at War*, to the Third Reich. But, with this war, there are apparently no goodies to cheer on. "In the Soviet Union and in America, the Cold War was fought by fear," explains the narrator, Kenneth Branagh. "The Soviet Union raised fences against the outside world. The Gulag, the secret universe of labor camps, swallowed the lives of millions. Both sides turned their fear inwards against their own people. They hunted the enemy within." As evidence of this, familiar images of the Eisenhower era drift by. "Leaders of the American Communist party were jailed, and the persecution spread. Left-wing labor organizations were banned, radical groups indicted, demonstrations broken up." That Stalin guy was an amateur compared to Joe McCarthy and Roy Cohn. These days, even the *New York Times* sheepishly concedes that Alger Hiss was, indeed, a spy, but *Cold War* presents him only as an early victim of Richard Nixon, "an ambitious young Republican." Say no more.

The House Un-American Activities Committee did not show America in its best light; it was in itself a very un-American activity. But, just for the record, those Communists who went to jail were convicted under the Smith Act for conspiracy to overthrow the United States government by force. It was the AFL-CIO—the equivalent of Britain's Trades Union Congress—which kicked out the Red-fronted labor organizations. And the Communist Party itself was never banned but continued to chug along, covertly funded by Moscow right up until the late 1980s. Ken and Jeremy at least feel the need to gloss discreetly over the unpleasantnesses—what exactly do they mean by "swallowed the lives of millions"?—but Ted Turner, founder of CNN , vice-chairman of Time-Warner and a gung ho pitchman for his series, is splendidly unrestrained. "We are often judgmental about people that are different from us," he says. "A lot of students got killed at Tiananmen Square, but I remember several students got killed at Kent State." In 1970, during an anti-Vietnam rally, four students died at Kent, shot by the Ohio National Guard. Rather more died at the hands of the Chinese, but Ted doesn't want to get into a numbers game. "Remember, they have a lot more students than us," he says. And, if there's one thing the world can always use less of, it's students. Ted, whose current Cause of the Week is population control, now says he regrets having five children. "But I can't shoot them now they're here," he sighs.

Last week, he was in Washington to address the National Family Planning and Reproductive Health Association but found time to return to the subject of the cold war, distilling the Isaacs approach into one casual aside: For President Reagan to call the Soviet Union an "evil empire" was, he declared, an "insult." Ted, of course, would never be so crass. Moving on to the pope's opposition to artificial birth control, he suggested the pontiff's disinclination to leave such matters to scientific gadgetry was typical of his people. "Ever seen a Polish mine detector?" he quipped, and then waggled his foot.

Turner's effusions on Tiananmen population control and Branagh's equation of a few underemployed screenwriters with Stalin's mountain of corpses are merely the more robust examples of the entertainment industry's enduring belief in "moral equivalence." Uncle Joe killed at least twice as many people as Hitler, not least because, as Ted would no doubt point out, the Russians had a lot more people. Still, we draw a distinction between the Nazis and the Commies—between the bad evil and the good evil, the evil that's philosophically sound, admirably progressive and just ran into one or two problems on the ground, like a great movie idea that went off course in development. Anne Applebaum pointed out the inconsistency in our views of the century's two great tyrannies in an essay for the recent book *The Future of the European Past*. But, in America, a couple of sniffy reviewers bemoaned the way conservative commentators are always bragging that they're the only ones who got communism right. It's true that, now that the Russians, the Romanians, the Albanians, the Mongols, even (tentatively) the Cubans have abandoned their faith in Marxist-Leninist orthodoxy, even America's diehard lefties are disinclined to speak up for the Soviet Union. But the proxy cold war being waged between

Kazan's defenders and detractors tells you where Hollywood's heart really lies: On Kazan's side are the syndicated columnist Richard Cohen, the *Toronto Sun*'s excellent Peter Worthington and, er, me; on the other side is everybody else. Kazan, says Thomas Oliphant in the *Boston Globe*, is "a pathetically prototypical rat-fink of the anticommunist hysteria." "He should be getting the Benedict Arnold award and the snitch-and-tell brass cross," says blacklisted filmmaker Abraham Polonsky. "When he goes to Dante's last circle in Hell, he'll sit right next to Judas." On that basis, Abe presumably will be sitting at the right hand of Jesus.

Still, while he can't do anything about the eternal damnation, Polonsky is prepared to call off the earthly tortures he'd lined up and drop the protests if Kazan apologizes. Don't hold your breath. "Apologize for what?" snorts the director's lawyer Flora Lasky. "Have these people apologized for supporting Stalinism and communism and the left wing . . . ? History has proved what communism was, and I expect that Mr. Kazan will simply say 'Thank you' in his speech."

Mrs. Lasky has a point. Why are people who are at best dupes, patsies, and obtuse clods so . . . revered? True, because of their "personal beliefs" their careers suffered; they were severely restricted in the practice of their craft. But every day around the world we restrict people from practicing their craft. In Britain, Glenn Hoddle is unable to practice his craft (such as it is) because of his "personal beliefs" about reincarnation. In British Columbia, the province's Human Rights Commission has just fined a columnist and his publishers and required them to run an apology in the paper because the guy inclines toward what we now call "Holocaust de-nial." Why should it be illegal to be an apologist for Hitler but socially acceptable to be an apologist for Stalin? Why should Kazan apologize to the apologists?

Well, say his critics, for one thing he betrayed his friends. The only commandment left in Bill Clinton's America is "Thou shalt not be a snitch-and-tell rat-fink"—a Linda Tripp or a Christopher Hitchens, who revealed details of a private lunch with White House aide Sidney Blumenthal. How could he do that to a friend? Is there anything so low? So Sid may not have told Chris the truth. Big deal. The proper response when your friend doesn't tell the truth is to stay loyal and keep quiet until you're either dead (Vince Foster, Jim McDougal), in jail (Susan McDougal, Web Hubbell,

Jim Guy Tucker), or drowning in legal bills (Betty Currie). That's friend-
ship.

Elia Kazan broke that rule, and with good reason. We are all entitled
to our "personal beliefs," and great artists are entitled to be forgiven more
than most: My respect for Tony Bennett is not diminished by the $10,000
he gave to the Clinton Legal Defense Fund. But what was at issue in 1952
was something more than "personal beliefs." "There was no way," wrote
Kazan in his 1988 autobiography, "I could go along with the crap that the
CP was nothing but another political party, like the Republicans and the
Democrats. I knew very well what it was—a thoroughly organized, worldwide conspiracy." The year after he testified, his friend Arthur Miller wrote
The Crucible, putting the work of the House committee on a par with the
paranoia of the Puritan witch-hunts. Even at the time, there were those
who pointed out to Miller the unsoundness of the metaphor: Witches, by
and large, didn't exist, whereas Communists did—and recently opened
KGB files tend to support McCarthy's estimate of their numbers rather
than Miller's. "The spirit of McCarthyism, the smearing of dissent as
communist treason," Kenneth Branagh intones solemnly on *Cold War*,
"stained American democracy for decades." Dissenters? Alger Hiss? The
Rosenbergs? This wasn't a difference of opinion. The "anticommunist
hysteria," says Democratic senator Daniel Patrick Moynihan, "did not
amount to persecution, still less delusion. Not a few in fact were spies."

This was the reality of the postwar world: The Communists very nearly
grabbed Greece and Italy; in 1945, the Soviet stooges seized Poland; in
1946, Bulgaria; in 1947, Hungary and Romania; 1948, Czechoslovakia;
1949, China. It would not have been necessary for the United States to go
communist. It would have been enough to have fallen into the feeble
stewardship of a Willy ("Détente") Brandt or a Pierre ("Viva Castro!")
Trudeau: You can figure for yourself how the cold war would have played
out. Only because America held firm could Europe and Canada afford to
indulge their natural wimpiness. It's easy to be loyal to friends, harder to
be loyal to those you don't know—rude peasants in exotic lands you'll
never visit, all the little people in those parts of the United States far from
Hollywood and Broadway where communism has no glamour. Whatever
his motives, Elia Kazan kept faith with his countrymen: He was on the

right side. We don't need to ask "Are you now or have you ever been a member of the Communist Party?" We know the answer to that. So a more important question arises: "Why?" And forty-seven years on, the "victims" of the "anticommunist hysteria" still cannot give us a credible answer.

15

Watching the Cold War

John L. Harper

John L. Harper is a professor of American foreign policy at Johns Hopkins University, Bologna Center, Italy. This article first appeared in *Survival*, April 1, 1999. Copyright Oxford University Press (England), spring 1999. Reprinted by permission.

At the Goodwill Games in St. Petersberg, Russia, in August 1994, CNN owner Ted Turner told his staff that the end of the cold war should be marked by the telling of its story. He gave the job to Jeremy Isaacs, producer of Turner's favorite documentary series, *World at War*. Sparing no expense, Isaacs's company assembled a team of writers that included Taylor Downing, Neil Ascherson, Hella Pick, Jerome Kuehl, and William Shawcross, scoured film archives around the world, and conducted five hundred interviews of protagonists and eyewitnesses from all sides and all walks of life. As its main academic advisers the series retained John Lewis Gaddis of Yale, Lawrence Freedman of King's College, London, and Vladimir Zubok of the National Security Archive, Washington, D.C.

Each forty-six-minute episode (eleven of which had appeared on CNN and BBC2 by early 1999) is a skillful weaving together of archival film footage, contemporary newsreels, and snippets of the specially commissioned interviews. The full texts of the interviews are to be made available on-line and will become a valuable scholarly resource. Maps are used effectively to illustrate many of the cold war's military campaigns and territorial disputes. The narration (read by Kenneth Branagh) is spare, trenchant, and concise. The musical score augments the sense, variously, of tension, drama, and pathos. The pace is brisk.

What the series conveys vividly is the gritty texture of the cold war struggle. In "Comrades, 1917–1945," for example, newsreels and archival film show us the war and wartime conferences, including the images and voices of Hitler, Stalin, Roosevelt, Churchill, and Truman. The interviewees include George Kennan of the U.S. embassy in Moscow, and his British counterpart Sir Frank Roberts, U.S. presidential advisers Clark

Clifford and George Elsey, as well as former Soviet officials Vladimir Yerofeyez and Sergio Beria. Beria (son of the notorious Lavrenti, chief of the secret police) describes how he spied on Roosevelt at Tehran. Ordinary U.S. and Soviet soldiers tell what it was like to meet each other on the River Elbe, and a Red Army photographer describes how he stitched together the hammer and sickle flag that was raised over Berlin. The narrative cuts through the controversy surrounding the Allies conference at Yalta by reminding us of "battlefield facts that diplomacy could not alter."

In "The Marshall Plan, 1947–52," Dimitri Sukanhov of the Soviet Foreign Ministry recounts Moscow's initial interest in Marshall's offer. Antonin Sum, private secretary to Jan Masaryk at the Czechoslovak Foreign Ministry, recalls the latter's July 1947 words: "I went to Moscow as the foreign minister of an independent sovereign state; I returned as a Soviet slave." A communist militant, a devout Catholic engaged to marry an excommunicated Communist, and a former CIA agent (who delivered "bags of money"), all evoke the "clash of civilizations" that was the Italian election campaign of 1948. A Greek peasant recalls his gratitude at receiving a hefty Missouri mule through the Marshall Plan. Giovanni Agnelli of Fiat describes what America represented at the time.

"Korea" vividly recounts a conflict that brought unbelievable suffering and destruction before the battle lines ended up where they had begun. In it a South Korean soldier recalls heading north in 1950 with "high hopes," and an American colonel relives the worst rout in U.S. military history. John Glenn (the astronaut and senator) describes piloting an F-86 against Soviet MiG fighters near the Yalu River. A Chinese veteran sings the song that accompanied his army's southward march. The wife of an American prisoner of war describes the climate of sullen disinterest toward the war that developed in the United States. In "After Stalin, 1953–56," we see a huge red star crashing into the street in Budapest and a secret policeman strung up by the neck. An Eisenhower administration official recalls, meanwhile, why Washington did not really want uprisings in the East.

Walt Rostow and McGeorge Bundy (aides to U.S. president John F. Kennedy), Raymond Garthoff of the U.S. State Department, Valentin Falin and Oleg Troyanovski (advisers to Soviet premier Khrushchev), and

West German politician Egon Bahr recount the high politics of the building of the Berlin Wall ("The Wall"). They make the point that Kennedy's
July 1961 speech signaled to Khrushchev that although the United States
would fight to defend Western rights, it did not intend to interfere with
what the Russians and East Germans did on their side of the line. Troyanovski aptly notes that, given the economic crisis of East Germany and
the failure of Soviet ultimatums, "The wall was a way out for Khrushchev."
Analysis is interspersed with the dramatic testimony of those who actually
built the wall, escaped across it, and nearly fought a tank battle over it in
October 1961. One of the most heartrending moments of the series is a
Berlin woman's account of how Peter Fechter, a young East Berliner shot
while trying to cross the wall, was allowed to die in a pool of blood as no
one interfered.

Conspicuously absent from these documentaries are historians, political scientists or other "talking heads." Isaacs insisted on making way for
eyewitnesses, some of whom may not be around much longer and most
of whom have not written books. The point, in other words, was to convey
to younger generations how the cold war, and its various "hot wars,"
affected the lives of ordinary people — "what it was like to be there" — rather
than to photograph the (ever-changing) state of the academic debate. In
this the series brilliantly succeeds. For accuracy and up-to-date scholarship
the series relied on its distinguished team of advisers as well as briefing
books prepared by the National Security Archive and the bulletins of the
Cold War International History Project based in Washington D.C.

Isaacs's approach was bound to provoke controversy. The memories
of protagonists are notoriously fallible. The minimalist narrative inevitably
ignores some events, oversimplifies others, and tends to gloss over long-
standing controversies. Not surprisingly, specialists have had a field day,
charging sloppy or obsolete or biased scholarship — or all three. For example, some would dispute the view (in "The Iron Curtain, 1945–47")
that the United States was extending its power all over the world; hence,
"Stalin grew nervous" and put pressure on the Turks to give him a base
on the Dardenelles. It is simplistic to say (as in "The Marshall Plan") that
European "industry lay in ruins" in 1945. Only about 15 percent of German and Italian industry was ruined — the more urgent problems were raw
materials and infrastructure — and Europe made great strides *before* the

Marshall Plan. In general, the series is Eurocentric and, within Europe, Berlin-centric (two of the first ten episodes deal with that city). It largely ignores events in the Far East except Korea and Vietnam. By the same token, it does not deal with the fundamental impact of the Korean War on European relations with the United States.

The choice (in "Vietnam") of former State Department official Roger Hilsman as the sole commentator on the U.S. role in the overthrow of South Vietnamese president Diem was misguided. Hilsman is widely considered to be one of the instigators of the coup. The episode pays too much attention to the unproved claim that Richard Nixon's entourage told the South Vietnamese to stonewall on a settlement pending the outcome of the 1968 U.S. presidential elections. One would have liked to have a more searching explanation of why American officials defined the U.S. interest in Vietnam and elsewhere in the Third World in the way that they did. Given the long-standing obsession of analysts with the October 1962 Cuban missile crisis, it is no surprise that "Cuba, 1959–62" has been picked apart. Indeed, the episode (including interviews with President Fidel Castro, Soviet ambassador to the United States Anatoly Dobrynin, Oleg Troyanovski, U.S. secretary of defense Robert McNamara, Special Counsel to President Kennedy Theodore Sorenson, head of intelligence in the U.S. State Department Roger Hilsman, Kennedy's press secretary Pierre Salinger, and Anatoly Gribkov, the Soviet commanding officer on the spot) runs roughshod over the chronology of events by implying that the crisis suddenly erupted on October 14, 1962. In fact the CIA had photographed surface-to-air missile sites in August, and Kennedy had issued a public warning on September 4. The episode does not make clear that Bobby Kennedy and Dobrynin had broached the topic of U.S. missiles in Turkey before October 27 and that President Kennedy was prepared to accept a public trade (under U.N. auspices) if Khrushchev had rejected his private assurances that the U.S. missiles would be removed. Philip Zelikow has argued that the episode ignores the latest findings on the crisis, namely, that Khrushchev, by installing offensive weapons, was thinking about Berlin; righting the intercontinental ballistic missile imbalance was a secondary consideration and deterring a U.S. invasion of Cuba hardly crossed his mind. This argument (echoing that put forward by Adam Ulam in *The Rivals*) will only spur new debate.

Certainly one would like to know why Khrushchev and Dobrynin did not raise the supposedly central Berlin issue during the critical moments of the affair.

The series makes the point that both sides were responsible for the arms race and the prolongation of the cold war, but there is little moralizing or triumphalizing about events. This no doubt reflects the influence of Turner, whose wish is to let bygones be bygones as far as the United States and Russia are concerned. And why beat a dead horse? The images (Stalin's camps, dead Hungarian freedom fighters, the barbed-wire-covered wall) as well as the Eastern bloc commentators, speak for themselves. The Korean War, says a former Soviet official, represented "a defeat for social-ism." The Berlin Wall, concludes the (East) German writer Stefan Heym, was "a symbol of defeat, of inferiority." This did not satisfy neoconservative critics. Charles Krauthammer, among others, seized on the episode "Reds," which juxtaposes a segment on McCarthyism with one on the contemporaneous Eastern European show trials. At the beginning of "Reds" the narrator says, "Both sides turned their fear inwards against their own people. They hunted the enemy within." In other words, writes Krau-thammer, "In the Soviet Union it produced the Gulag; in the United States, the red scare. Half the show on one, half on the other. This is moral equivalence with a sledgehammer." Among his specific complaints are that Julius and Ethel Rosenbergs' crimes (they were executed as Soviet spies) are not spelled out: "A high-schooler watching this might imagine they passed a picture of a power plant to a Soviet attaché."

In fact the Rosenbergs were small-fry compared to other atomic spies. More important, it would be a dull high schooler indeed who concluded from "Reds" that the two systems were morally equivalent or that this is what the producers were trying to get the viewer to believe. The narrator tells us that "in the Soviet Union all dissent was suppressed." While Stalin survived "it meant death to disobey him." The Gulag "devoured the lives of millions." Both Isaacs and John Gaddis have replied to Krauthammer. It is hard to argue with Gaddis on this point when he says that "the tapes speak for themselves."

A more telling criticism, surely, is that the series tends to portray the past forty-five years as a time of unmitigated troubles for humanity, a long parentheses of terror from which we have been lucky to escape. The subtitle of the lavishly illustrated book accompanying the video set is *For 45 Years the World Held Its Breath.* (The book might have been called *The Cold War on Your Coffee Table.*) It is true that there were millions of casualties and several brushes with nuclear annihilation. The book is good on the near-disastrous accidents involving nuclear weapons that were closely guarded secrets at the time (RAF Lakenheath in 1957, North Carolina in 1961, Thule, Greenland in 1968).

But in that time there has also been unprecedented prosperity in the Western world, a solution to the German question, and the flowering of European integration with U.S. encouragement. In Central and Eastern Europe there was no freedom, but life there (except in Czechoslovakia, 1918–38) was no picnic before the Soviets arrived. The superpowers were able to compromise when it counted to avoid a third world war, at times against the wishes of their respective allies—a point that the series makes effectively. The cold war "system" was not a U.S.-Soviet condominium. It was, to use Gaddis's phrase, a long peace. Will the post–cold war world be as safe and rich as the world of 1945–1989? Let us hope and pray.

16

Televising the Cold War

Thomas Doherty

Thomas Doherty is an associate professor of film studies at Brandeis University and author of *Projections of War: Hollywood, American Culture, and World War II* (1993). This article first appeared in the *Chronicle of Higher Education*, April 2, 1999. Copyright *Chronicle of Higher Education*, April 2, 1999. All rights reserved.

In scope, ambition, and cost, CNN's twenty-four-part *Cold War* may be the most formidable documentary series ever screened on television. Bankrolled by Time Warner and produced by a team of veteran filmmakers from Thames Television and the BBC, the project aspires to become the definitive visual record of the bipolar postwar world, the chronicle of choice on the great twilight struggle between capitalism and communism, the individual and the collective, the United States and the Soviet Union. Premiering September [1998] and telecast weekly through Sunday, April 4, it already has been deemed a "landmark documentary" by . . . , well, by the teasers for the series on CNN.

Cold War is a timely, high-profile exemplar of a genre that has itself thrived in the postwar world: the "video doc," a made-for-TV documentary that makes a montage from pictures of the past. Arriving punctually at century's end, *Cold War* proves again that, in the age of the moving image, history on film is almost always more dynamic and influential than history in books. Lent an imprimatur from CNN, PBS, or the History Channel, anchored by the lulling tones of an authoritative baritone voice-over, any video doc—no matter how compromised, simpleminded, or downright wrong—leaves an indelible imprint on popular impressions of the past.

From the high-tech glitz of its trademark opening (a scene shot moving through a tunnel with East and West images on either wall) to the musical leitmotif that punctuates each segment (a prolonged, shrill note on a lone violin), CNN's polished contribution to the genre reflects both the promise and the problems of history-making television.

Certainly the workaday pressures of American education have conspired to extend the cultural impact of the video doc. Teachers seeking a shot of classroom adrenaline (or craving a respite from a killing work schedule) can simply pop a cassette in the VCR and—voilà—an instant lesson plan. For their part, the networks and cable channels have found in the video doc a congenial blend of prestige and commerce.

Compared to other shows, documentaries are cost-effective: The sets are already built, and the stars are either people who had been unpretentious eyewitnesses to history (grateful to tell their story to solicitous interviewers) or obscure experts (often academics only too happy to secure some face time on television). Even the real talents, the name-brand actors who narrate the action or re-create the characters, are willing to work cheap for the privilege of assuming the voice of God. After broadcast, the sponsor then peddles the documentary package to libraries, educators, and videotape outlets, usually with a slick coffee-table book as ancillary marketing.

At its best (as in Ken Burns's nine-part *The Civil War*, produced in 1990 for PBS), the video doc melds sharp images, seamless editing, and trenchant commentary to make a distant world appear up close and personal. At its worst (as in WNET's notorious *Liberators: Fighting on Two Fronts in World War II*, produced in 1992), it can be an embarrassing and duplicitous cut-and-paste job. In falsely crediting African American troops with liberating the concentration camps at Dachau and Buchenwald, *Liberators* demeaned the stellar combat record of the black troops it purported to honor.

CNN 's model for *Cold War* was Thames Television's famed *The World at War* (1974), the magisterial documentary record of World War II. An authentic landmark in the merging of film and history, still replayed incessantly on cable and public broadcasting stations, the Thames series set the gold standard for the video doc genre. It pioneered and perfected many now-conventional techniques: the aloof recitation of the most awesome and awful happenings (intoned by a British actor with a Shakespearean pedigree), the dual perspectives of former battlefield combatants brought face-to-face on film, and the equal weight accorded "talking heads" from both headquarters and the combat lines.

CNN's founder, Ted Turner, a longtime admirer of *The World at War*, recruited the executive producer of that series, Sir Jeremy Isaacs, to work the same magic for *Cold War* (hence Turner's credit for "series concept" after each episode). With Turner as patron, Sir Jeremy and his production chief, Martin Smith, possessed the kind of budget and resources that most documentarians can only fantasize about. By all accounts, Turner took a hands-off approach, but he did lay down one ground rule: The internationalist-minded media mogul decreed that, in chronicling the fall of the Soviet empire, the series should avoid any hint of American "triumphalism."

The *Cold War*, which CNN's narrator, Kenneth Branagh, dubs "the first multimedia war," is exceptionally well suited to the video doc. Unlike World War II, the progress of which was seen on newsreels projected days or weeks after the fact, many of the epochal events of the cold war were broadcast in real time, simultaneously with their unfolding: Joseph McCarthy's flameout at the army-McCarthy hearings in 1954, John F. Kennedy's bracing speech to the nation during the Cuban missile crisis in 1962, the fury of Vietnam, the ceremonies of summit diplomacy, and— the thrilling climax to the war—the collapse of the Berlin Wall on live television, a truly global spectacle.

For many of today's viewers, who beheld so many cold war touchstones live on television, the replaying of history has special vividness and force, often unleashing a chain of sometimes unnerving flashbacks. (The first time around, remember, a network news bulletin on some of the events would disrupt regularly scheduled programming, just possibly advising you to prepare to meet your maker.)

Not that *Cold War* is merely a video trip down memory lane. Spectacular film footage not seen previously—the best of it acquired from the archives of the former Soviet Union—enlivens almost every episode. Like many totalitarian regimes, the Soviets took an intense interest in film as a medium for political persuasion and social control. "The cinema is for us the most important of the arts," Lenin famously remarked. Yet, with the exception of censored newsreel footage and a handful of Politburo-approved feature films cleared for overseas export, little of the Soviet motion picture trove was ever viewed in the West (or in the East, for that matter). Now new film footage is being unearthed from the storage vaults of Kremlin bureaucracies—everything from home movies of Tsar Nicholas II to launch pad catastrophes of the Soviet space program. (A source of some of the best footage has been the KGB, which kept a file copy of anything that caught its eye.) Another contribution to cold war dramas is the way that the CNN series lets its characters speak with particular, and very human, emotional power. Soviet policymakers, witnesses, and victims can now talk on camera without fear of reprisal. By juxtaposing different speakers, East meets West in shared memories of the Berlin blockade, *Sputnik*, espionage, and rock 'n' roll. Throughout *Cold War*, the producers slyly insinuate a cinematic sense of dialogue by shooting the Western witnesses facing screen right (east) and the Soviet witnesses facing screen left (west). That is light-years away from cold war video docs once broadcast by the American networks, which brandished titles like *Nightmare in Red* (1955) and *Meet Comrade Student* (1962): When *Cold War* parts the Iron Curtain, the folks behind it look quite friendly, really, even if some are rather poorly attired.

Nevertheless, since it is the cold war that CNN is documenting, controversy comes with the territory. With the real cold war over, the tense face-offs between rival ideologies have shifted to the academic front, and, lately, the scholarly battles have been heating up. The once-dominant "revisionist" view, articulated by new left historians bred in the 1960s and traumatized by Vietnam, has ceded pride of place to an aggressive revision of that revisionism. Where the old revisionists viewed the cold war as a scam that served the imperial interests of both sides, and especially the political ambitions of American anti-Communists, the outlook of the new revisionists is summed up by the title of a reappraisal by the historian Richard Gid Powers, *Not Without Honor: The History of American Anticommunism* (1995).

The opening up of archival records in the Soviet Union and the declassification of top-secret American documents (notably the Venona files, decoded intercepts of Soviet intelligence traffic) have given the new cold warriors some powerful ammunition. Together, the disclosure of Soviet and American secrets has done for cold war historiography what the discovery of the Dead Sea Scrolls did for biblical scholarship: recast and revitalized a moribund discipline. The recently published *Haunted Wood: Soviet Espionage in America—the Stalin Era*, by the American historian Allen Weinstein and former KGB agent Alexander Vassiliev, draws extensively on the Venona files and KGB archives to demonstrate the degree of Soviet penetration into some of the highest levels of U. S. government. Reviewing the volume in the *New York Times*, another historian, Joseph E. Persico, compared reading the recent cold war scholarship to "looking into a new edition of a book from which half the pages had previously been torn out." The same could be said of watching video docs like *Cold War*: It is like looking at a restored film from which the best footage had previously been left on the cutting room floor.

Predictably, the narrative arc and thematic drift of *Cold War*—like the recent scholarship—have sparked a torrent of skirmishes. "Tendentious," snarled the *New Republic*'s Jacob Heilbrunn, lambasting CNN's presentation of the cold war as "a morally ambiguous contest between two equally dangerous superpowers." Over at the *Nation*, the problem was that *Cold War* presented the conflict as too morally unambiguous. "The Cold War was about Europe, Americans responded effectively and we won it: The good guys defeated the bad guys even if the cost was often excessive," the historian Bruce Cumings sardonically noted in his review of the CNN series. If nothing else, the critical response to the documentary proves that bipolarity, if finished in geopolitics, survives at home.

In fact, throughout CNN's *Cold War*, what seems to be at stake in the struggle is not so much human freedom as the survival of the species. The postwar menace is less the Soviet Union and communism than thermonuclear annihilation. Even the Berlin Wall looms more as a mutual failure in communication than the supreme symbol of the Soviet state as a prison camp. With some justice, the fiercest criticism of *Cold War* has targeted episode six, "Reds: 1947–1953," an all-too-impartial survey of the crimes of two cold war Josephs: McCarthy, the reckless junior senator from Wisconsin, and Stalin, the genocidal maniac from Georgia. The hour-long show equitably divides the two tales of domestic oppression into two evenly parceled segments of screen time, where the hundreds dragged before congressional committees are paired with the millions shipped off to the Gulag.

Whatever the flaws of the series, such is the power and shelf life of the video doc that CNN's *Cold War* may well be the best-remembered version of history's cold war. On balance, it is a meritorious look back at a period when words like apocalypse, extinction, and Armageddon defined military scenarios more often than movie plots. Set against the model of *The World at War*, however, *Cold War* is hobbled by its pose as a disinterested spectator. What made *The World at War* so compelling was not just the charismatic witnesses and stunning archival footage but the moral trajectory of the historical narrative. Each episode underscored the theme of how evil thrived because good men did nothing; of how, through great struggle and painful sacrifice, the evil was ultimately vanquished.

Cold War duly notes that one of the superpowers won the war, but in avoiding "triumphalism" it too often forgets why the West had a rooting interest in the home team.

17

Broadcasting History

Lawrence Freedman

Lawrence Freedman was one of the three principal historical advisers to the CNN series. This article first appeared in *Prospect*, June 1999. *Prospect* magazine is a London-based monthly whose web site can be found at www.prospect-magazine.co.uk.

The twenty-four-part BBC 2 series the *Cold War*, which has now drawn to a close, has been greeted respectfully, even enthusiastically, by critics and academics in Britain. There was a time when academics steered clear of such ventures, fearing for their scholarly reputations. But I am happy to say, as a historical consultant to the series, that most historians now recognize the professionalism of our best documentary makers and the importance of film to the historical record. The combination of archive footage and interviews with participants in the events of the period was considered too traditional by some and the pace too slow by others, but few in Britain have doubted the seriousness of Jeremy Isaacs's team.

Not so in the United States, where the series has been broadcast by CNN. There it has been subjected to withering criticism, mainly from neoconservative journals such as *Commentary*. For them, attempts to present the Soviet point of view or draw attention to the less admirable aspects of U.S. conduct is to indulge in "moral equivalence," suggesting that the two superpowers were equally to blame for the cold war breaking out in the first place and persisting for as long as it did.

This basic charge is made by Jacob Heilbrunn in the *New Republic*. There are two ways to view the cold war, he claims: either as "a justifiable (if sometimes excessive) American struggle to contain, and ultimately defeat, a monstrous system that was intent on global expansion"; or as "a morally unintelligible contest between two equally dangerous superpowers, whose fear of each other threatened to plunge a world full of innocent bystanders into nuclear holocaust."

The rottenness and ultimate failure of the communist system is a matter of record. Nobody is going to come away from watching the *Cold*

War thinking it a shame that the confrontation was not declared a draw. My own position during the cold war was never revisionist. I was convinced that communism was a malign ideology, rendered more dangerous by the backing of Soviet power, and that this required a determined response from liberal democracies. This did not mean that I lost all sense of proportion when considering Soviet policy. We can now look back with some detachment; pick up on the misperceptions of the period; and acknowledge moments of great danger when the world really was on the edge of catastrophe.

The neoconservative perspective was never very strong in Europe during the cold war itself. For Europeans the confrontation was, at one level, much more real. On this divided continent Soviet power exercised a palpable influence. Europe's stability depended on the close involvement of the United States in its affairs. This was never easy. The Americans were asked to take substantial risks on behalf of allies who did not always show gratitude. Europeans found dependence uncomfortable and worried constantly that they would be abandoned or dragged into an unnecessary conflagration through American recklessness.

They were made particularly nervous by those militant views that came to be associated with the neoconservatives. Anxiety levels could always be raised in Europe by suggesting that a way could be found to win a nuclear war. Neoconservative claims that the Moscow gerontocracy was still bent on world domination, or that the presence of communist sympathizers in a Central American nationalist movement justified making common cause with vicious forms of repression, did enormous damage to America's image, especially during the early years of the Reagan administration, when their influence was at its height.

It is therefore not surprising that they now denounce a series that fails to give them what they consider to be their due in bringing about the collapse of the Soviet empire. The burden of military rivalry, which they did their utmost to intensify, was clearly one reason why the Soviet state failed. But the most important reason was the constant demonstration that in terms of prosperity as well as freedom the Western system was superior. This was reinforced by many of the East-West contacts undertaken in the name of détente, usually deplored by neoconservatives.

Despite *Commentary*'s headline—"Twenty-four Lies about the Cold

War"—the producers were scrupulous in their effort to get their facts right. There are unavoidable issues of balance and interpretation. A program that has to deal with McCarthyism and the Gulag may create an impression of equivalence—but only for someone who ignores the commentary and the evidence presented. Elsewhere, images of accidents at Soviet factories or KGB interrogations brought home the brutal nature of the system.

One of the achievments of the series was to gain access to stunning Soviet film archives as well as interviews with former Soviet officials. If this opportunity had not been taken it might have been lost forever, given the recent deterioration in the West's relations with Russia. Critics object to giving old apparatchiks the chance to explain themselves. Yet the authenticity of their voices remains beyond doubt, and to hear them can make sense of actions that would otherwise appear inexplicable.

The problems with any series such as this tend to result not from bias, but from the limitations of the medium. Television can do things that the written word cannot, by conveying the humanity of the participants and the images and sounds of the past. But they are dependent on those stories that are either well-told by interviewees or well-covered by film archives. They need to hold the attention of viewers who can always switch over. So good stories told badly, or events unrecorded, get passed by. Most of all, time is limited. A television script is a fraction of the length of a modest academic article. Points are made starkly, with little scope for nuance. For all these reason, the *Cold War* is not the final word on the cold war. Few of those involved would agree with every word. Moreover, historians are still working their way through the archives. But the series has provided a coherent record of events that shaped our world.

18

The War That Left Sir Jeremy Cold

David Wilson

David Wilson is writing a history of the journal *Encounter*. This article first appeared in the London *Spectator*, May 15, 1999.

BBC's twenty-four-part series *Cold War*, produced by Jeremy Isaacs for Ted Turner's CNN, has just ended. The ambition of Sir Jeremy Isaacs, whose *The World at War* was one of the classics of televised history, was to bring what he calls "the central story of our times" to life.

Cold War is narrated in sententious tones by Kenneth Branagh. "For forty-five years the world held its breath. An epic story told on a human scale," which says more about the production values of CNN than the quality of its historical advisers. Judging from the interviews given by Isaacs in the initial publicity campaign, the production team took great pains to come to some kind of consensus on cold war historiography. Nevertheless, they reached no settled conclusion on what the conflict was actually "about."

Isaacs has, somewhat unwittingly, entered into one of the most heated controversies in the United States: the debate, raging for decades, between "traditionalists" (broadly pro-Western) and "revisionists" (often believers in the moral equivalence of the West and the communist world, and commonly pro-Soviet) on the nature of the cold war.

Isaacs compared the editors of the neoconservative American monthly *Commentary*—whose review article was pointedly titled "Twenty-four Lies about the Cold War"—with those of *Pravda*. Isaacs has said, time and time again, that Turner did not want a "triumphalist" series and that it was his conscious intention to avoid "vainglorious and victor's history."

The *Cold War* scripts have tended toward the "revisionist" approach, emphasizing a general equivalency between the two superpowers, which is odd, given the unequivocally anti-Soviet views of the senior historical adviser on the series—the American, John Lewis Gaddis. Debates involving Gaddis and his critics have filled academic journals for the last twenty-five years. His revisionist opponents like to portray him as the McCarthyite "gatekeeper" of cold war history. Gaddis has wearily demurred that the debate was capable of "eliciting torrents of impassioned prose, of inducting normally placid professors to behave like gladiators at scholarly meetings, of provoking calls for the suppression of unpopular views, threats of law-suits, and most shocking of all, the checking of footnotes."

It is not just generals who always fight the last war; intellectuals do little else. This makes it all the more extraordinary that, until recently, the war of ideologues has been discounted by commentators. The honorable exception to this "no first premises" rule were the writers gathered around the now defunct journal *Encounter,* and they, for the most part, were dismissed as "professional cold war warriors."

The *Cold War* scripts, however, were written by a different breed of authors, including Ian Buruma, Germaine Greer, Hugh O'Shaughnessy, Jonathan Steele, and William Shawcross, and, first among scribbling equals, the Old Etonian radical journalist Neal Ascherson. If one were to think of a generic term for them it would be "aging sixties radicals"— "committed" people who cut their teeth on demos protesting against the Vietnam War. Marx once said that when the locomotive of history turns a corner, all the intellectuals fall off. It is not altogether the revisionists' fault if they now find themselves in the railway sidings of history. Yet some things remain eternal and the Stars and Stripes is still the most burnable of flags.

The first episode of *Cold War,* entitled "Comrades, 1917–45," ludi-crously claims great popular support for the October revolution (in actu-ality a Bolshevik coup d'état): Orlando Figes's insistence that it was a people's tragedy is ignored. Ascherson's script cravenly ducks Lenin's re-sponsibility for the totalitarian nature of the Soviet state; there is no in-dictment of Leninism as an ideology that enslaved; rather he falls back on the cliché of a "revolution betrayed." But as the great Russian historian V. O. Kliuchevski has written, "the state swelled up, and the people grew lean."

The episode on the postwar division of Europe, "Iron Curtain: 1945–47," also written by Ascherson, portrays an otherwise pacific Stalin's Russia "growing nervous" as the United States attempted unilaterally to "extend its influence and power all over the world and was consequently forced to build its own rival bloc." Given that this "rival bloc" already existed and given that the Red Army did not so much liberate Eastern Europe as rape, pillage, and murder its way through the entire Soviet zone of occupation — might not the West be forgiven for "growing nervous" in response to the extent of Soviet "influence"? Stalin's insistence on surrounding himself with utterly subservient states is glossed over.

The portrait of Truman that emerges from the successive episodes is the hackneyed one of the "parochial nationalist" who "lacked the patience to weigh up the subtleties of arguments" and was "largely ignorant of foreign affairs." This is Stone Age history. Truman, it is now widely acknowledged, was one of the great foreign policy presidents, who acceded to office determined to honor the Yalta accords, but who was forced to construct Nato and the Truman Doctrine to put a brake on Stalin's expansionism. However, the narration characterizes the Truman Doctrine as constituting the "official declaration of the Cold War." Molotov later recalled that "Stalin looked at it this way. World War I had wrestled one country from capitalist slavery; World War II had created a socialist system; and the third will finish off imperialism forever."

Nowhere in the series is the question of why the conciliatory policies of détente and arms control of Nixon, Ford, and Carter were accompanied by a massive Soviet military buildup and an expansionism that culminated in Afghanistan's invasion. Reagan, of course, is depicted as the "acting president," an imbecilic cowboy driven by "an irrational fear of communism."

If excuses can be made for the television series no such waivers can be made for the accompanying book, also called *Cold War*. Oleg Gordievsky was surely right in naming it as the worst book of last year. While it has pretensions to high seriousness, it makes no attempt to engage with the historiographical debate and lazily pushes an unexamined "revisionist" line.

The one general history by a Western academic recommended in its bibliography is Gaddis's own *We Now Know: Rethinking Cold War History* (1997). *We Now Know* is an awe-inspiring synthesis of the latest published research and documentary material newly unearthed from the Soviet archives, but it is, unfortunately, a book that no one connected with *Cold War* appears to have read. Although *We Now Know* is meant to be a provisional account, nevertheless it is heavy with the kind of historical certainty that Ted Turner would term "triumphalist."

Gaddis insists that the West won because of the moral superiority of liberal democracy and capitalism's efficacy. But because of the paradoxical legacy of McCarthyism within the American academic community, it is a view that does not carry universal respect. Gaddis writes: "The excesses of the 1950s so traumatized us that, by the time I entered graduate school in the mid-1960s, to talk about the ideological roots of Soviet foreign policy was to sound a bit like a member of the John Birch Society, if not Tail Gunner Joe himself."

Gaddis condemns the USSR, China, and their acolytes as the true originators, escalators, and perpetuators of the conflict. Moreover, he argues that Western scholars have traditionally underemphasized the role of ideology—both the vibrancy of Western liberalism and the redundancy of Marxist-Leninism. Gaddis places the moral barbarity of Stalin's Soviet Union at the heart of the cold war and argues that the West's role in resisting Soviet expansionism should initiate a reappreciation among historians of the moral necessity and strategic utility of containment.

That Lenin's Leviathan was both politically illegitimate and historically contingent, the general viewer would get no clear idea from *Cold War*. Although the end of the cold war was not the "end of history," as Fukuyama has called it, it was the end of Soviet history. Yet *Cold War* is dominated by a discredited balance-of-power, spheres-of-influence view of the conflict: a morally equivalent approach in which two armed camps simply fought each other to a standstill in a meaningless struggle for global supremacy. In Turner's parallel universe, to reduce tensions it was only necessary to understand the concerns of the adversary and act accordingly. Which is where Gorbachev comes in.

We now know that though the Soviet empire collapsed with its superpower strategic capability intact, a steady deterioration in its nonmilitary resources—economic, cultural, and moral—had left it gangrenous in its guts, leaving the deus ex machina that was the Gorbachev phenomenon an irrelevant specter at the wake. Gorbachev wanted to end the cold war in order to regenerate the Soviet state; instead, the Cold War ended with the demise of the whole Soviet system. George F. Kennan, then U.S. chargé d'affaires in Stalin's Moscow, in his famous pseudonymous "Mr.

X" article, concluded, as early as 1947, that the USSR was comparable to Thomas Mann's Buddenbrooks family. Mann observed that human institutions often show outward brilliance at a moment when inner decay is furthest advanced, like "one of those stars whose light shines most brightly when in reality it has long ceased to exist."

The last word should go to Ted Turner. "We are often judgmental about people that are different from us. . . . And we don't even understand what their problems are. A lot of students got killed at Tiananmen Square, but I remember several students got killed at Kent State. And, remember, [the Chinese] have a lot more students than we do." As that terrible old historicist Hegel mournfully observed, historical forces trample down many a flower. Who now remembers the victims of Yalta?